THE WITNESS OF BROTHER JOHN

The Testimony of Brother John

Printed in the U.S.A.
Library of Congress

1.Religion

Printed in the United States

Contents

A LIGHT IN A DREAM FROM AN IMPORTANT VISITOR

I dreamt that I was in my house and through the window I could see a light slowly coming up my long driveway and I felt intuitively that the person carrying the light was a very important person. I thought, this person is going to be here soon and my house is not in order!

Still asleep, I got up and ran to my window. When I finally awoke, I found myself staring out my bedroom window at a streetlight across the street.

The dream reminded me of the gospel of Jesus Christ and how Jesus warns us to watch, "Lest coming suddenly he finds you sleeping." Mark 13:36

CHAPTER 1 – LEARNING TO LISTEN TO GOD

Two weeks before the Christmas of 1976 I made the decision to stay home and pray and fast for the first time in my life instead of going to my parents home for the traditional celebration. Before starting this fast I read and prayed the prayer I had found in the 'Four Spiritual Law' tract I'd received two weeks earlier from the son of a neighborhood pastor. Having been granted a three day holiday from my job this Christmas, I was alone with God on Christmas Eve. No one knocked at the door, and no one called on the phone. For almost three days I did not even go downstairs.

On December 27, 1 9 7 6 I returned to my job, and, looking back, it was a day that went unusually smooth. In the evening I went to the Danta Society for my daily meditation. I was sitting in meditation when the thought came to me that if life is so empty, why live? I caught this negative thought, and told myself I should be focusing on positive thoughts. So I asked myself, what is the most positive thought I can have? Then, straight out of the blue, these words came to me, "Be ye therefore perfect, even as your Father which is in heaven is perfect" Matt. 5:48. I recognized it as coming from the Bible but I had never memorized it! I thought, if the Word of God bids us to be perfect, then it must be possible to be perfect. Yes! That's a very positive thought. I *can* be perfect! Then the thought came to me, is there a more positive thought than, I can be perfect? Suddenly I thought, I *will* be perfect!

But again the thought came to me, what thought is even more positive still? Instantly, I thought, I *am* perfect! And when I had that thought, I was given the first vision in my life.

I saw in my mind's eye what appeared to be monks sitting in a circle at my feet. In the vision I was standing, and I was wearing a white robe, long hair and beard. My hands were slightly lifted out from my sides palms forward. We were in a beautiful green meadow with the sun shining gold as in an autumn sunset. The monks sat in a circle. They sat perfectly still, and love and kindness shone from their faces.

About five years later, I wrote this Poem describing the above vision.

THE IMAGE

In a meadow sat they all so still
Together love shining from their face
With September's Sun shining gold
The verdure reflecting golden green

These have found the one they sought
Ne'er will they e'er look apart
For this one answered to that need
That longed so deep within their heart

Encircled sat they at their master's feet
Happy to see him in their midst

This happiness beaming from their face
Watching not to miss a single word

There stood their master in glistering white
The very image of perfectness sublime
Yea, the very image of the Christ
Yet I knew the face to be mine!

As a result of this vision I felt God was making good his promise of perfection to me through His Son. "But as many as received him, to them gave He power to become the sons of God, even to them that believe on His name." John 1: 12. Also, "Whereby are given unto us exceeding great and precious promises: that by these ye might be partakers of the divine nature…"   (2 Peter1:4) KJV   After this vision, there came a sense of well-being that gradually and gently grew stronger and stronger.

Other brothers in the meditation room began to rise and leave, I was in such a state of ecstasy, I loathed to stir, but out of concern for drawing unwanted attention to myself, I also, arose to leave. But just as I was crossing the threshold I recalled a most wondrous dream I had had the night after my holiday chastening.

I heard a voice saying, "LET ME SEE YOUR WORK." The sound or tone of this voice was the most remarkable part of the whole dream, because it was the most clear, even toned, serene, and tranquil voice I had ever heard, before or since. The tone of this voice was so penetrating in its serenity that it created a profound sense of well-being and security, resonating at the very core of my being. In obedience to the voice, I went over to an object resembling an ice box and opened it. It was clean and white inside. Then the voice said, "NOW REMOVE THE COVER."

I then pulled out a white false bottom, and underneath was blackness with what appeared to be insects swarming and scurrying from the light. Suddenly one of the insects came floating out, and as it came closer, I realized it was actually a scorpion full of fury and venom. The scorpion appeared to be trying to sting itself to death. I was horrified because it was flying straight at me. Then as quick as lightning, a kind of transparent white ghost came out of my left side. The ghost was dressed like a monk in a white robe and having no hair.

His person and robe were all of one color that of monofilament nylon fishing line, a kind of transparent white. The ghost, as quick as lightning, stretched forth his arm, and out of his index finger shot a transparent white ray of light that coiled around the scorpion. Then clear drops began dripping from the scorpion and onto a transparent black floor and became hardened drops.

Then there arose fumes from these drops reeking of an alcoholic's bad breath, and the stench of a dirty ashtray all rolled into one nauseous stench. All the things from

8

which I had recently quit doing miraculously without much effort. Then the scorpion settled down and began to weep. The ghost went to the scorpion and wiped the tears from the scorpion's eyes. Then he wiped the scorpion's whole body down, mounted the scorpion, and rode off into the sunset.

I went home and straight to my room so I could be alone with my wonderful new sense of well-being and peace. I was so happy and full of joy that I kept thanking the founders of the Danta Society because I thought this Hindu religion was the source of all of this wonderful grace! I felt God very close to me, and so I said out loud, "God I love you!", then in my Mind's ear came a reply like a loud thought, "kill thyself!".

I was shocked and perplexed, but then I thought perhaps I could find out the meaning of this strange demand by seeking a dialogue with this voice. So I said, "God I love you!". Again the voice said, "kill thyself". So then I ventured to inquire and asked, "What do you mean kill myself?". The voice answered, "Destroy your ego!". Then I gathered that it meant that I was to live a self-denying life rather than actual suicide.

Then the thought came to me that I really ought to inform my guru about this wonderful new transformational experience. But alas, when I told my guru he did not seem to understand. Rather than rejoicing with me, he angrily said, " You shouldn't ever tell your dreams to

9

anyone." I was totally shocked by my guru's strange reaction and lack of mutual feeling.

This led me to question the source of this wonderful flood of grace and truth. Then I recalled that about a month before Christmas, I opened the Bible my brother Allen, gave me and in the introduction, it promised that I would receive plenary indulgence if I prayerfully read the Bible for twenty minutes a day for thirty days, which I did.

Years later, having heard the testimonies of other Christians, I saw that the single most important act that led to my being born again was the act of prayerfully studying the Word of God with a sincere intention of practicing the Word. Is that a single act?

I had also recalled the pastor's son, who had given me the "Four Spiritual Law" tract, and had told me the Bible said I could come closer to God by accepting that Jesus Christ took my punishment for sin. It was becoming clear that the source of all this grace was not from the Danta Society and my guru, but the grace and peace I felt was coming from Jesus Christ!

More than forty years later, I see that meditation was also very important in getting me started on my spiritual quest and in keeping me on the straight and narrow path.

This experience was so soul-shaking and life-changing that the thought of returning to my job as day doorman at the hotel, filled me with horror because the atmosphere was so worldly and I didn't want to be tempted. I felt compelled to call the hotel. I informed them I was leaving, and I never returned.

I had a girl friend who wanted to marry me, I was not in love with her, nor was she a Christian. I had been trying to break off the relationship, but she would always come back to tempt me. After this great change of heart, when she came to tempt me this time I was filled with horror. Now when I saw her, I saw sin and death. I calmly rose my right hand and pointing at her and said, "In the name of the Jesus Christ, get out." She immediately turned and ran away—cursing me as she went. Shouting over her shoulder, "You're selfish and no good!"

She never returned to tempt me again. I now had a new self-control and my fear of death was gone, along with my fear of man. I no longer feared what men thought of me because I knew that I was secure in God's love. Before this experience, I was terrified of speaking in front of an audience. Now I still experienced a certain apprehension which resulted in a kind of quaking when I spoke in front of a group, but this quaking only had the effect of making the audience all the more attentive seeing my earnestness and sincerity.

"And I say unto you my friends, be not afraid of them that kill the body, and after that have no more they can do. But I fore warn you whom ye shall fear: Fear him, which after he hath killed hath power to cast into hell: yea, I say unto you, fear him." Luke 12: 4-5 KJV

A new revelation came to me that was so radical I was reluctant to share it. The revelation was that the established state and traditional churches were not really the true invisible and indivisible church of Jesus Christ, but were in reality, of the world and agents of the state. It suddenly became abundantly clear to me this present world is as upside down as it was when Jesus walked the earth, and that it was the rulers and state that crucified Jesus. It was officialdom that crucified Jesus, and martyred the saints. In the last days a one world government will be given power to fight and overcome the true saints. "And it was given unto him to make war with the saints, and to overcome them: and power was given him over all kindreds, and tongues, and nations." Revelation 13: 7.

My outlook toward what was real and true shifted so dramatically that I began to think that either I was going insane or the whole world is under a great and all encompassing delusion! "And we know we are of God, and the whole world lieth in wickedness." I John 5:19 "...for thy merchants were the great men of the earth; for by thy sorceries (pharmakia) were all nations deceived." Revelation 18: 23. And again, "And for this cause God shall send them strong delusion, that they should believe a lie." 2 Thessalonians 2:11. And again, "I also will choose their delusions, and I will bring their fears upon them: because when I called, and none did answer: when I spake, they did not hear: but they did evil before mine eyes, and chose that in which I delighted not." Isaiah 66: 4. And again, "For false Christs and false prophets shall rise, and shall show signs and wonders, to seduce, if it were possible, even the elect." Mark 13:22. And finally, "...the great dragon was cast out, that old serpent, called the Devil, and Satan, which deceiveth the whole world." Revelation 12: 9.

What most impressed me was that if I was not watchful to continue fasting and praying, I too, would gradually fall back again under the same diabolical spell of darknes Satan has the whole world under. And I would become forgetful of God and preoccupied with the cares of this life, as is the world. Jesus said, "Take heed to yourselves, lest at any time your hearts be overcharged with surfeiting, and drunkness, and the cares of this life, and so that day come upon you unawares." Luke 21:34. And also, "He also that received seed among the thorns is he that hearth the word; and the cares of this world, and the deceitfulness of riches, choke the word, and he becometh unfruitful." Matthew 13:22

And Saint Paul wrote, " But they that will be rich fall into temptation and a snare and into many foolish and hurtful lusts, which drown men in destruction and perdition. For the love of money is the root of all evil: which while some have coveted after, they have erred from the faith, and pierced themselves through with many sorrows. But thou, O man of God, flee these things; and follow after righteousness, godliness, faith, love, patience, a n d meekness." 1Timothy 6: 9-11.

One day, about a month after this radical revelation, a book on a shelf caught my attention. The book was entitled, 1001 Dreams Interpreted which reminded me of my regeneration dream with the scorpion.

I looked in the index under scorpion since the scorpion was one of the most dominate symbols in that dream. It said, to the best of my recollection, "If you see a scorpion in a dream and do not kill it, then it means that a false friend is about to deceive you, and you are about to lose a lot of money."

At this point in my new walk with Jesus, I was being led to renounce all of my property and money. So this horrified me. But then I thought, it's the words of Jesus leading me to sell all and distribute to the poor, and I know that Jesus is not a false friend. Then it occurred to me I did not know the author of the book I was holding in my hand, and I dropped it as I was filled with a feeling of revulsion and horror. I immediately searched the entire house to find all such occult books. After finding a surprisingly large number of these books, I threw them all into the garbage.

I started attending classes for the baptism of the Holy Spirit. At the end of six weeks the class received prayer with the laying on of hands. Afterward, I had a season of prayer. After this period the Holy Spirit began to speak to me about the power of united prayer and fasting by showing me that the Church was started at Pentecost with united prayer and fasting. I felt the presence of God so intensely that I could not sleep, save for an hour in the morning. But during the night, I suddenly felt I should try to speak in tongues and I simply opened my mouth.

14

And without any real effort, a few strange sounding words came tumbling out. I felt like a child and wept. I also felt a stirring in my breast, but the stirring didn't stop, it continued to climb up my middle to the root of my tongue then to the tip of my tongue then finally I felt a tingling sensation on the tip of my lips.

I was led to read from the Bible. I turned to the book of Luke and read: "And why call ye me Lord Lord and do not the things which I say? Whosoever cometh to me and heareth my sayings, and doeth them, I will show you to whom he is like: He is like a man which built an house, and digged deep, and laid the foundation on a rock: and when the flood arose, the stream beat vehemently upon that house, and could not shake it: for it was founded upon a rock. But he that heareth, and doeth not, is like a man that without a foundation built an house upon the earth; against which the stream did beat vehemently, and immediately it fell: and the ruin of that house was great." Luke 6:46-49.

I felt that the Holy Spirit was informing me that I was a fundamentalist Christian and not to be ashamed of it, because a fundamentalist is nothing more than a doer of the Word

CHAPTER 2 - THE TRAPPIST ABBEY

It was the Spring 1977, a few months after my conversion,
I had taken in a boarder, a divorced man. This man's
children came to visit him one Sunday and made such a
noise that I could not bear the disturbance. I left the house
almost at a run heading for a monastery a friend had told
me about. I was in such a hurry to get out of the noisy
house that I didn't take the time to tell them I was
coming, nor did I know exactly where this monastery was
located. I knew only the name of a nearby town. I took
the city bus to the Portland Greyhound bus station, and
then took the regional bus to a certain quaint farm town of
Oregon. I got off the bus and found the road leading to
the monastery which was indicated by a small sign that
read, " ABBEY". The size of the sign gave me the
impression that these monks were hiding, and there was
nothing indicating how far I would need to walk with my
luggage. However, it was a beautiful rural setting and a
lovely spring day. It was afternoon when I had gotten
thus far.

When I finally arrived at the Abbey, which I found
tucked away almost out of sight in beautifully wooded
gently rolling hills, it was twilight. I was trusting God that
there would be an accommodation even though I had not
madeany reservations. As I began walking up the long
gently curving drive, fearful thoughts of being turned
away began to assail my mind. Despite these fearful
thoughts I had an idyllic walk in the somber twilight, the
still misty air, the lush green of spring. In concert with

the scenic beauty was the sound of nature's music, a medley of chirping crickets and croaking frogs in the roadside bog.

They did have a room for me, though humble, it was quaint. I recall being grateful to have anything after so long a walk into a kind of unknowingness. But then it was just such experiences, a kind of walking on water as it were, that left me utterly enchanted.

Moreover, it was at just such times that I most felt the presence and nearness of God, and I could best see the hand of providence at work turning people's hearts to help.
"Behold, his soul which is lifted up is not upright in him: but the just shall live by his faith." Habakkuk 2:4.

During my visit to the Forest Abbey, I was in prayer saying my penance after confession. One of the Fathers took my confession and told me for my penance to imagine myself saint Peter after he had denied Jesus three times. So I began to imagine that Jesus is asking me, "John, lovest thou me?" I said, "Yes Lord I love you."

Then Jesus said, "Join this monastery." I was so shocked by such an unexpected demand that I nearly forgot what I was about when suddenly I was awakened from my total absorption in thought with the words, "John, do you love me?"

I answered, "Yes Lord I love you." The voice replied, "Return to the Catholic Church."

This shocked and perplexed me even more and feelings of suspicion and doubt began to fill my mind so much so that I again nearly forgot what I was supposed to be doing. When suddenly I was brought back by the words, "John do you love me?"

I answered, "Yes Lord I love you." And the reply came, "Trust me."

The next day I made an appointment to tell the Abbott that I felt the Holy Spirit is calling me to join the Abbey. Now I should explain that since my conversion experience I had grown uncommonly fond of fasting and praying and one of the effects of all this fasting was an attitude that was intensely zealous, fearless, and guileless.

This attitude, understandably, made most people ill at ease around me. Something I was almost totally unaware of. Now the Abbott has never met me, and doesn't know me from Adam. So the first thing I ask the Abbott is, how many of the monks have communion with God?!
T h e Abbott replied, "Well that depends on what you mean by communion with God." Then I ask him for his testimony. Again the Abbott is at an apparent loss for words, and does not quite seem to know what I mean by testimony. I gave him a short version of my testimony so as to give him an idea of what I meant.

When it became his turn to give his testimony he seemed to squirm and gave me the impression that he did not really want to give his testimony. I did not press him any further. Then I told the Abbott of my recent experience and that I felt that the Holy Spirit was calling me to the Abbey, and that I did not understand why God would call me return back to the Roman Catholic Church! I said that perhaps God was calling me to become another Martin Luther to bring reform to the Church.

By this time the Abbott is beginning to take a definite disliking to me, and even begins to wonder if I am insane. But alas, I only realize this much later. The Abbott tells me to return home and join my local parish, and to come back in one year.

Before leaving the Abbey I had yet another indelible experience. I was praying in the main chapel and I do not recall speaking any words, but I recall at least forming the idea of the monastic life in my mind, and while praying to myself, I thought, "God I love you so much, I believe I could live the life of a monk." Instantly, the clouds broke, and a shaft of light streamed through one of the high overhead chapel windows. I sensed that the shaft of light and its timing meant something important had transpired. I only learned many years later, while reading the most beautiful Christian testimony of Aimee Semple McPherson, that the shaft of light was the seal of God!

When I prayed, "God I love you so much, I believe I could live the life of a monk." God took my words as a solemn vow!

19

It took me almost forty years to understand this. Satan has tried many times to stumble me, but God has kept me these forty years. "For he shall give his angels charge over thee, to keep thee in all thy ways." Ps. 91:11 Thank you Jesus!

Easter sunrise 1977 I was baptized by my brother Allen in the Columbia River at Rooster Rock, Oregon. Allen's wife Teresa took a photo of Allen and I as we came back from the river, but when she developed the photo we were not there. Perhaps because we were too distant and there was insufficient light.

CHAPTER 3 - THE GIFT OF PROPHECY

During the summer of 1977 I was living at home with my parents and joined their parish, All Saints Catholic Church. At a prayer meeting I learned about an organization called, Loaves and Fishes, a nutritional program for the elderly and shut-ins. Delivering meals for them eventually led me to one of their centers on skid row. Through prayer meetings and my sister Pat I learnd about the charismatic movement in the Catholic Church. I began attending these meetings and felt they were more meaningful than the formal liturgy of the mass. The meetings were being held at the University of Portland campus. The leader was a Jesuit priest who takes a disliking to me. At one point he told me if everyone read their Bibles as often as I did he would forbid them to bring their Bibles!

I had asked him a number of times if I could give my testimony, but he would always put me off with the reason that he didn't think I was quite ready. He never did give me an opportunity to give my testimony.

I started attending classes for the baptism of the Holy Spirit. At the end of six weeks the class received prayer with the laying on of hands. Afterward, I had a season of prayer. After this period the Holy Spirit began to speak to me about the power of united prayer and fasting by showing me that the Church was started at Pentecost with united prayer and fasting. I felt the presence of God so intensely that I could not sleep, save for an hour in the morning. But during the night I suddenly felt I should try to speak in tongues and I simply opened my mouth. And without any real effort a few strange sounding words came tumbling out. I felt like a child and wept. I also felt a stirring in my breast, but the stirring didn't stop, it continued to climb up my middle to the root of my tongue then to the tip of my tongue then finally I felt a tingling sensation on the tips of my lips.

Then I was led to read from the Bible. I turned to the book of Luke and read: "And why call ye me Lord Lord and do not the things which I say? Whosoever cometh to me and heareth my sayings, and doeth them, I will show you to whom he is like: He is like a man which built an house, and digged deep, and laid the foundation on a rock: and when the flood arose,the stream beat vehemently upon that house, and could not shake it: for it was founded upon a rock. But he that heareth, and doeth not, is like a man that without a foundation built an house upon the earth; against which the stream did beat vehemently, and immediately it fell: and the ruin of that house was great." Luke 6:46-49.

At this point I felt that the Holy Spirit was telling me that I was a fundamentalist Christian and not to be ashamed of it, Because a fundamentalist is nothing more than a doer of the Word.

That evening I went with my brother to his church. During the meeting I was brimming over with enthusiasm and a very positive feeling to speak and tell the people about the Holy Spirit. How that the established "Church" does not give the Holy Spirit his rightful place or reverence, but is rather swept under the rug and given a back seat. But since there was no call for testimonies I waited and spoke to the pastor instead. The pastor responded by saying that if he proposed baptism in the Holy Spirit, the church would split in half.

Curiously enough this church split in half anyway over who was going to be the pastor. Our conversation turned toward the poor and I learned that the pastor had a different idea about who the poor were. I opened my Bible and showed him that the Bible tells us what is meant by the poor, that we do not have to speculate. I read:The Spirit of the Lord is upon me, because he hath anointed me to preach the gospel to the poor; he hath sent me to heal the broken hearted, to preach deliverance to the captives, and recovering of sight to the blind, to set at liberty them that are bruised, to preach the acceptable year of the LORD." Luke 4:18-19.

When the pastor began to feel the weight of the passage he tried to find fault with the translation, but when I showed him it was a King James Version of the Bible, he became slightly flustered. He said that he had spent many years studying to qualify himself in these things, and that I was too young to speak in the Church. I did not recall this at the time, but the Holy Spirit brings it to mind now how that, "Jesus rejoiced in spirit and said I thank thee, O Father, LORD of heaven and earth, thou has hid these

things from the wise and prudent, and hast revealed them unto babes."
Luke10:21

The next morning I went to church with my mother. During the scripture reading I was
in a kind of reverie when suddenly I was shocked to attention when I heard the priest read, "Then said I Ah, Lord God I cannot speak for I am a child. But the Lord said unto me, Say not, I am a child: for thou shalt go to all that I shall send thee, and whatsoever I shall command thee thou shalt speak." Jeremiah 1:6-7. This reading reminded me of what the pastor said to me that I was too young to speak in the church. I looked in the missalette to see and made a note that the reading was from the book of Jeremiah. I would study it closer when I could be alone.

Later at home I was in the bathroom brushing my teeth when I began thinking of the power of the Word of God, and the power of prayer. I began to rejoice when suddenly I remembered that I was going to study more closely the first chapter of Jeremiah.

When I came to Jeremiah 1:9 I read, "Then the Lord put forth his hand, and touched my mouth." Then suddenly I recalled how two nights before there was this stirring in my heart and how it continued up through my middle then through my tongue and finally left a tingling sensation on my lips. I suddenly realized the Holy Spirit had not only bestowed the gift of tongues upon me but the gift of prophecy as well! And now he was using this experience and the testimony of Jeremiah to seal or confirm the gift of prophecy. Hallelujah!

The Holy Spirit was showing me that he had anointed me as he had anointed Jeremiah. The realization of this and the presence of the LORD were felt so intensely that I fell on my knees and wept tears of joy and thanksgiving. And even now fifteen years later as I am writing this, (the original writing was done in November of 1990 while I was living in Israel) the Holy Spirit is showing me that my experience with my brother's pastor was a type of renactment of, or refulfillment of Luke 4:18-19.

Where it says, "The Spirit of the LORD is upon me, because he hath anointed me to preach the gospel to the poor; he hath sent me to heal the brokenhearted, to preach deliverance to the captives, and recovery of sight to the blind, to set at liberty them that are bruised, to preach the acceptable year of the LORD."

A short while after my born again experience, I had a waking vision. As I awoke I hear someone yahooing me. Calling to me, "Don Quixote, Don Quixote". I woke up wondering, what is this Don Quixote? I hadn't heard of this before. I went to Powell's Books down town Portland. I asked at information and they led me to a copy of the book. It is known as the first novel. I would call it an allegorical novel. I began reading it on the spot. Liked it and strongly identified with Don Quixote.

Later I looked up Cliff's Notes and found that some scholars see Don Quixote as a mad man and others see him as a Christ or Saint Frances of Assisi type. What I found most interesting is some see the allegory as a kind of mystical mirror. What one sees when they read Don Quixote is what they themselves are!

Many years later, I learned that there was a Movie "Man of La Mancha". I recognized the title and thought I should watch it. I did not get around to it until Frank a good friend of mine said to me, "John, you have to see this Movie "Man of La Mancha". He exclaimed, "It's you! It's you!" We watched it together and Frank was right it is me and it became our favorite movie.

On December 27, 1977 I went to a prayer meeting. When I arrived, I could not resist telling them that it was my birthday. My born again birthday that is. Then one of the nuns exclaimed, "That is interesting because today is Saint John's feast day! I for one do not believe in coincidence.

CHAPTER 4 - THE PILGRIMAGE TO MADONA HOUSE

Most people would consider it fool hardy to hitch hike Trans Canada 1 in January, but this is what I feel the Holy Spirit is calling me to do. I have never hitchhiked long distance before, and now I am planning to hitch hike from Portland, Oregon, USA to Pembroke, Ontario, Canada, a distance of roughly two thousand five hundred miles!

I start this trek in the dead of winter without proper cold weather clothing, knowing that I will be traveling through sub-zero weather. To top it all off, I feel the Holy Spirit is telling me to take no money. Not even a penny! Some would say this is tempting fate, but during this experience, I learn many things. Most importantly how to trust God for provision and protection. Indeed, it is during such times as these that I feel the presents of God most. (Even now, as I write this forty years later, I feel the call to travel penniless again!)

When I sold all and renounced all of my property, it was not because I wanted to, but because this gospel passage kept going around in my head, "…sell all that thou hast, distribute unto the poor, and thou shalt have treasure in heaven: and come follow me." Luke 18:22 And when I started this pilgrimage of two thousand five hundred miles across Canada it was not because I wanted to, but I felt compelled to as I kept hearing the gospel passage go around in my head saying, "...take nothing for your journey, neither staves, nor scrip, neither bread, nor money; neither have two coats apiece." Luke 9:3

It was January 1, 1978 when I left home with only a vague idea of how I was to even get started on this very long adventure! As soon as I get packed and left the house it started snowing for the first time that winter. It didn't look encouraging, but I was determined. (As I write forty years later, I'm reminded of Don Quixote's first sally from his home, his was in the middle of summer. Mine was in the dead of winter.)

I had heard of a road ministry called Shiloh House and thought I had remembered where it was. So my first destination is a house at a distance that I should be able to manage within the same morning. The only problem was I did not know the address but only vaguely recalled the neighborhood where it was located.

As I begin to look for the house, I wonder if perhaps this house only exists in my imagination or I had only dreamt of it. I found the house after walking up and down a few streets and have a feeling of déjà vu, but more like a dream come true. It rhymes! As I approach the house, again I'm assailed, by all kinds of doubts and misgivings. I have never begged for a bed in my life, and they might turn me out in humiliation. A friend warned me that if I traveled without means I would be mistook for a "dope smoking hippy". Also, I had just turned thirty and I might be too old. So, when all these doubts assailed me, instead of walking straight up to the front door, I think to walk by slowly and do a kind of visual reconnoiter. I look at the front window and a friendly face of a young girl just happens to be looking out. I am encouraged by the friendly smile and turn around and cautiously approach the front door. To my surprise and delight, everyone is unusually warm and friendly. The house is warm and I can smell something good cooking in the kitchen.

The leadership ask me where I am from and to where I am traveling. When I tell them, they frankly admit that they have doubts about it being the God who is calling me to a place called Madonna House. They were right, but I needed to learn this for myself, and the LORD knew this.

That evening two young Canadian men come to Shiloh House who are also hitch hiking to Canada! The next morning, in four inches of snow, I show them to the nearest on ramp to Interstate 5 North. After trying to hitch for a while, there is talk of splitting up because of the difficulty of getting a ride with three men. But, shortly after this a van stops and takes all of us to Seattle. We split up in Seattle. I'm hitch hiking on I 5 when a police officer pulls up and tells me to get off the free-way.

I start walking to the nearest on ramp, but I get a ride before reaching it. This man's car has a flat and he has no spare! So, I start walking down the free-way again and it is beginning to get dark and it starts to snow and rain! I start to pray especially hard and looking to see if there are any signs of shelter. It is a rural area and I can see what looks like farm houses off in the distance. I begin to wonder again about this whole thing if God is truly in it. Then suddenly someone stops for me it is almost dark!

The man who picks me up is an American Indian from Canada and he gradually begins to tell John that he has just been released from prison. He tells me, "You are lucky to get a ride at such a late hour."

I thanked him very much for the ride. But, I begin to wonder what kind of company I have fallen in with. Then the Holy Spirit reminds me that this man needs to hear the gospel of Jesus Christ. So, I tell him my testimony. I find this man to be fairly open but he has been wronged and oppressed a lot by white man and finds it difficult to trust in white man's religion.

By the time we get to the U. S. and Canadian border we are fairly well acquainted the man knows I am not a Canadian and have no money. He tells me that if border police find out that I have no money, they will turn me back. I decided to simply tell the authorities where I am going and show them the letters they sent me and let God work out the details come what may.

When we approach the Canadian side, we pull up to the border patrol window while I am half asleep but mentally prepared to fill out the forms and answer the questions. But, instead of the American Indian pulling up to the offices to do paper work, he continues down the highway. He turned to me and said, "You know, I just lied for you. They asked if you were a Canadian citizen and I said, yes."

I was shocked, I told him that he didn't have to lie for me and that I was perfectly willing to speak for myself and be turned back if that was God's will.

My new friend drives on to Vancouver, British Columbia Canada and drops me off and I don't know where I'm going to spend the night.

 I went to the nearest store to borrow a phone but the store keeper was unkind to me. I wondered why he was being so unkind when he didn't even know me. Then I recalled what Gary Grove told me about being mistaken for a dope -smoking hippy. So, I went to a phone booth and I looked in the telephone directory and find a Shiloh House listed! I had anticipated needing change for phone calls but can't recall who gave me the change but there it was in my pocket! So then I call the Shiloh House and they give me directions.

When I finally arrive, I am treated warmly but with reserve as though they are not sure if they can trust me. The head of the house talks to me and I speak to him about self-denial. The head of the house disagrees with me and says that self-denial should not be over-emphasized.   I said, the real danger is not in over-emphasizing   self-denial but in under-emphasizing self-denial. At this juncture, I could see that the leader was quite angry but was trying to hide it. After dinner, I volunteered to help with washing the dishes and while washing the dishes I shared my testimony with the other man helping.

Then the leader walks in and says he wants to talk to me privately and tells me I will have to stop preaching or leave. I said, "I am not preaching, I'm simply sharing my testimony."

The leader says, "No, you are preaching. And you will have to stop or you'll have to leave."

I decide that I do not want to stay in a place where I'm not even allowed to share my testimony. After getting directions to another shelter, I leave.

At the other shelter, I bump into the other two Canadians I started traveling with in Portland! They are unusually glad to see me as though it was a good omen. They had some bad luck after splitting up with me and from this they'd deduced that by sticking close to me, they would have better luck in getting rides.

The next morning we are a trio again. A van picks us up and gives us a ride to Hope, British Columbia, Canada where we spend the night at a Hostel. The Hostel manager asked me if I had any money and I tell him no. Then he asked the other two Canadians if they had any money of which they also said, No! I knew they were lying because I knew they had some money. This got me to thinking if I really wanted to keep traveling with these two Canadians. I decided I would part ways at first opportunity.

This opportunity comes in the morning. The Canadian guys slept in late and I wanted to get an early start.

After a short time, I got a ride going all the way to Calgary Canada. Late in the afternoon, I take the wheel to drive for a while. Everything is going fine until we start getting more and more into the Rocky Mountains. It starts snowing and night falls.

At this point, I should have let my host drive. But, I wanted to earn my keep as it were and loathed to quit driving. It's snowing and there is a slow moving tanker in my way, so I try to pass. I get around the tanker, no problem. Then I come to a down-grade in the road and I want to slow down so I decelerate. But unknown to me there is black ice on the road just at this spot and the car begins to fishtail.

I look at my host and my host looks at me. The car starts to fishtail even more, until we are doing complete donuts in the oncoming lane! The car bounces off the snow bank on the wrong side of the highway and slides back over to our lane, hits the snow bank, and rolls over on its top! The car continues to slide like a sled until it finally comes to the bottom of the hill and comes to a smooth and gentle stop. Thank God, we both have our seat belt and shoulder harnesses on. There we were sitting upside down on the side of the highway. My host starts yelling: "Turn off the ignition! Turn off the ignition!" I fumbled for the ignition, and turn it off and the motor dies. All I could think was, "Thank you God we didn't get killed by oncoming traffic."

Here we are hanging in our seat belts and shoulder harnesses upside down. Getting out of these when the car is right side up can be difficult, but imagine trying to get out of these when you are upside down!

We both managed to get out and by this time many people have stopped and are running to our rescue. The help we need is to push the car ride side up. There are so many men to help and the car is only a small Datsun. So this is easily done. Then my host quickly pushes the top that had caved in back out and takes the wheel.

All the men push the car back onto the highway and in only about five minutes we are sailing down the highway again, almost as though nothing had happened. But something had happened and my host was now in an unusually sour mood. Mostly, because his car's body was a total wreck.

He takes me to his brother's house and from there he takes me to the nearest emergency shelter, which is so over-crowded with drunks that I have to sit all night in the hallway with nothing. This place was like a very over-crowded mad house. I would have gladly slept outside but it was twenty degrees below zero and this is the first time I have ever been in weather this cold.

This is how I managed to hitchhike in subzero weather. I would find a place to hitch from and quickly find a public building I could run into when I felt I was reaching the limits to the bitter cold.

I remember the first such public building was a super-market. The thing that struck me most about Calgary was its booming economy and how its people all seemed to be money mad. On TV, everyone was watching some kind of lottery where the winners struck it rich. In the super-markets there were huge banners everywhere telling their customers to sign up for the sweepstakes so they could have a chance to win something like a one million dollars.

Every time the police stopped me, they asked me if I had any money. That seemed like the most important question. But to this day, I still can't figure out why the police would always ask me that question because it never seemed to make any difference, perhaps if I had brought money they would have busted me for being in Canada without papers. (Now, I realize that since I didn't have papers, they would have busted me but only if I had had money.) I always told the police where I was going and showed them the letters from Madonna House.

For the next two weeks I didn't know how I would get my next meal or where I would sleep the next night.

Generally, I went from one major city to the next and stayed in emergency shelters from Calgary to Regina to Winnipeg to Thunder Bay. When I got to Ontario and near Lake Superior the temperature warmed up about fifty degrees! From about thirty degrees below zero to about 20 degrees above.

When I arrived in Thunder Bay, there were huge piles of snow in the super-market parking lot, I was getting out of the car and pulling my coat around me bracing for the cold. When I stepped out of the car, I was surprised. I'll never forget I was so surprised because I was ready for the cold weather to bite me but instead it felt almost tropical. It was twenty-five degrees, still well below freezing and it felt almost tropical. What a pleasant surprise. I had to unzip my coat!

Every time I got a ride long enough to tell my testimony, I would. I realized it was a perfect time to witness because it would usually be one on one and a captive audience.

Sometimes, my witness would result in a very short ride, but that was ok, because it would always resulted in a better ride.

When I arrived at Pembroke Ontario, a town about 12 miles from Madonna House, it is midnight and twenty degrees below zero. I didn't want to stay at the truck stop, so I go out on the highway to hitchhike, when a deputy sheriff pulls up in his car and asks me, "Where do you think you're going?" I am not sure how to answer at first, so I ask him, "Are there any emergency shelters in Pembroke. The deputy sheriff answers that Pembroke is too small but I can have a jail cell if I want.

 I decide a jail cell beats freezing and going without any rest. I hop into the car and get a free ride and a free bed. The only problem was that the jail door was locked and my bed was a steel bed with no bedding, not even a mattress and the light was left on all night with cameras aimed straight into my cell. I didn't rest very easy that night. The next morning they let me go with no breakfast of course. I am encouraged though because I'm thinking I will probably make it to Madonna House on this day.

My first impression of Madonna House is positive. Indeed the place is as beautiful and as enchanting as Camelot. Eventually though, I see by the Holy Spirit the pagan idolatry of Russian Orthodoxy and Roman Catholicism. The Madonna House was a hodge-podge mix of Russian Orthodoxy and Roman Catholicism. I am assigned the job of supplying wood to the cottages and maintaining the out houses in the morning and was assigned odd jobs in the afternoon. The food was excellent and I noticed I had to be careful because I was starting to put on weight.

I would exhort everyone to read the Bible more because although this was supposed to be a religious community virtually no one paid much attention to the word of God and prayer! I am introduced to the founders of the Madonna House, Catherine Doherty. She asked me why I had come to Madonna House, I answered, "The Lord told me to come."

She replied, "Well, I know that, but for what in particular?"

I said, "I'd heard about the Madonna House ministry through Catholic friends and had read one of her books and had come to learn how to pray."

Catherine said, "Oh, well, that's simple!"

I answered, "Yeah, simple but not easy."

Catherine said, "Well, I didn't say it was easy."

Once again, I began to speak on self-denial and Catherine Doherty does not like it any better than the man at the Shiloh House who told me to leave.

One day I felt led to pray to open the Bible and pray at random for a special word from the Holy Spirit. I close my eyes and pray and open my Bible at random where I see in my mind's-eye the four columns of my Bible and were it is dark and shadowed is where I start reading. "Sanctify ye a fast, call a solemn assembly, gather the elders and all the inhabitants of the land into the house of the Lord your God, and cry unto the Lord…" Joel 1: 14.

I began to get the very definite impression that the Holy Spirit wanted me to call a fast at Madonna House. So I prayed, "Lord, if this really is You, give me a sign?"

Then the next day, I opened my Bible at random again and I began to read where it was shadowed. "Sanctify ye a fast…"

Miraculously, I had gotten the very same passage. Now, in the flesh, I did not want to talk to Catherine Doherty about this but I felt so strongly about this in the Spirit, it would not let me rest. So, I asked to see Catherine Doherty but learned she was on holiday in the Bahamas and wouldn't be back until about a week before Easter. I told the leadership there at Madonna House that I would like to speak with Catherine when she returned.

One night, in the men's dorm, one of the other men asked me, "Why does the leadership here treat you differently?"

I asked, "What do you mean?"

He replied, "Well, I over-heard them having a meeting and they were talking about you."

I admitted that this was curious, but also had to admit I was not sure why I was the subject of discussion at the leadership council meeting. However, whenever such incidents happened, the Holy Spirit would remind me, "These things have I spoken unto you, that you should not be offended. They shall put you out of the synagogues, even killing you, thinking they are doing God service. And they will do these things because they know not My Father, nor Me." John 16:1-2.

Another such passage the Holy Spirit would bring to my mind at such times was, "Blessed are you, when men shall revile you, and persecute you, and say all manner of evil against you falsely, for my sake. Rejoice, and be exceedingly glad: for great is your reward in heaven: for so persecuted they the prophets which were before you." Matthew 5:11-12.

Catherine Doherty finally arrives back from her one month holiday in the Bahamas about two weeks before Easter. I get an appointment to speak with her. I tell her that I believe that God wants the community to pray and fast before Easter.

She asked me, "How long have you been at Madonna House?"

I answered, "About three months."
She says, "You can bring your ideas when you've been here longer. Don't bring this subject up again until I tell you."

CHAPTER 5 - A YOUNG MAN PLANNING SUICIDE

Early February 1978, I am still at Madonna House, but not feeling so welcome and beginning to make plans to visit my Uncle Brother Ferdinand at Our Lady of Gethsemane. We were in the Main building and it was evening and they were getting ready to watch a movie called *The Shoes of The Fisherman* starring Anthony Quinn. I was torn because I had not seen any movies since my born-again experience and I was tempted to stay, because it was warm inside and outside it was 20° below zero. They were serving refreshments and there were many social activities inside the building tempting me to stay. However, the thought came to me to go outside to a workshop a short distance. Denying my flesh I fled.

At the workshop, I prayed and the thought came to me that I might find a kindred spirit who is also serious about prayer if I go over to the chapel instead of going to the movie. I left the workshop and as I trudged along toward the chapel. The spotlight above the chapel door seemed to be beckoning me onward.

When I went inside, I looked for boots, hats and coats, but I did not see any so I assumed I was alone. I noticed the lights were off and normally they were all on. I got ready to shout aloud "Praise the Lord!" but just before I did someone else shouted out from the dark, "Who's there?" Then he came out of the shadows so I could see him. He was a young skinny man and it looked like there were ashes on him. He asked me, "Who sent you?" The thought came to me, be slow to speak and quick to hear. Then he said again, "Who sent you?" Then he said, "The reason I keep asking who sent you is because I was planning to commit suicide. I was praying to God for help and as soon as I finished my prayer, you walked in the door." I was stunned, but I realized that God had sent me to this young man.

He said he had come there for counseling and was trying to get off drugs and he said that he felt like Jesus. I told him, "I think you might be having a born-again experience." He said the leadership at Madonna House told him they could not help him and were going to put him on the next bus out. He could not understand why they would not help. I told him that true and faithful Christians are far and few between I wished I had shared with him more of my thoughts of how I was led to the chapel to make it more clear to him that I was indeed miraculously sent. I prayed with him. I then left and he remained in the Chapel.

At breakfast, the next morning, he walked into the dining hall. He looked unusually scared and insecure. I should have smiled and welcomed him to sit next to me, but since I knew that the leadership wanted him out, I did not! He sensed that I did not want him to sit next to me and he sat at another table.

The time for me to return to the Trappist Abbey Our Lady of Guadalupe was nearing, and I began to make plans for this. Before returning though, I thought I would make another visit to my uncle to the Trappist Abbey Our Lady of Gethsemane. I thought also that it might be good to pay a visit to the charismatic community in Ann Arbor Michigan. Especially, since this was supposedly where the charismatic movement began in the Catholic Church some five or six years earlier. When I arrived there, it was like a ghost town, neither could I find any good hospitality or any good explanation for the lack of it.

I am told, over the phone, I would have to go to the police first if I wanted accommodations. I went to the police station and told them I was looking for accommodations at the charismatic community called the Word of God, and that they had sent me there. After a long wait at the police station, I got someone on the phone. I took the phone and introduced myself, telling the man on the other end, who refused to introduce himself for security reasons, that I wanted to visit the Word of God charismatic community.

The man asked me, "Are you a Religious?" I replied that I was planning to enter the Trappist Abbey of Our Lady Guadalupe. This seemed to make a little difference. The man said that if I would go to such and such an address, I would find a motel that would give me accommodations for the night. This so far, in my experience was the most cagy and coolest hospitality I had, thus far, had received in my new walk with Jesus.

I was disappointed with this Word of God community and felt I had not enough time to look more into it. Therefore, the next morning I returned to Madonna House and met a priest who just happens to be going to visit Our Lady of Gethsemane. Great, my Father has provide me a ride all the way to Trappist Kentucky to Our Lady of Gethsemane to visit my uncle Bud whom I had visited about nine months earlier. A Trappist monk called Brother Ferdinand.

The first thing I thought I would do when I arrived at the Abbey was to go to confession. Therefore, I asked to see my Uncle Bud's confessor. After confession, I asked him, "How is Brother Ferdinand?" The last time I had seen my uncle was in July 1977 and he was in good health. When I asked, the priest's face fell and he said, "Haven't you heard?"

I said, "No, what?"

The priest said, "Brother Ferdinand passed away during Holy Week and we've just buried him."

This news caught me by total surprise. A sense of loneliness and loss came over me. The priest explained that I was the first of any relatives to visit even though his brother Joseph Burger had been informed. The priest also explained how he died suddenly from cancer only about a week after a visit to the hospital. I had written a letter to my uncle, but had received no reply. His illness and death, of course, explains why. Apparently, he was too sick to write.

I leave Our Lady of Gethsemane and head for Our Lady Guadalupe. On the way, I try to find the family property near Brookings Oregon. I had only a vague idea of where the property was so my first attempt is unsuccessful because I am on the wrong road going up the north bank of the river when I should have been going up the south bank of the river.

I hitchhike eight miles back into the wilderness. I can't find the property so I decided to just camp out on public property and it starts raining and I don't have a tent. Then it got dark and started raining even harder so I run into the forest looking for a large tree to hide under and get out of the rain and wind. I find a huge rotten log and lay close to its lee side. I was still getting wet because the water started dripping off the saturated log. So I dug away some of the loamy dirt to make a hole under the log. I cannot see them because it's dark, but I know I must be making my bed for the night in the midst of centipedes and many other worms and bugs.

I make it through the night without much sleep naturally. The morning brings sunny skies so I decide to stay even though I have no food. Then when night comes, it starts pouring down rain again even harder than the night before. This was more than I bargained for, and so as soon as morning light comes, I head for town.

On the road to town, I found some young people in a van. They gave me a lift into town, and even treated me to a bowl of soup. Apparently, they saw my plight. After this, I am ready to report back to the Trappist Abbey Our Lady of Guadalupe.

Hitchhiking through the rural part of the Willamette Valley in spring time is a wonderful experience. I could see why people call Willamette Valley God's country. I had left Interstate 5, and was on a particularly lovely country road. If my recollection serves me correct, it was part of the old highway 99 between Salem and McMinnville. I was walking along the road because I was finding it difficult to get rides. I was

44

determined to make it to the Abbey before nightfall, even if I had to walk the entire 25 miles or whatever the distance was.

As I walked along I saw a huge old Oak trees where a driveway met the road. I saw filbert orchards, apple orchards, walnut orchards, I saw almost every kind of fruit tree. But it was not the variety that struck me, it was the perfect temperature combined with the abundant fresh growth. The clean fresh air and the relative peace and quiet after having been on a dirty and noisy interstate highway for many hours. Also, there was something quaint and mellow about these orchards that is not found on many of the new and commercial truck farms that are so prevalent now days. Feelings of nostalgia swept over me as I recalled my childhood home and how I had taken my rural childhood home on Pleasant Valley Road for granted.

Now, I thank God for the wonderful memories for having been raised on a homestead in the country. The woods, fields, orchards, and pristine wooded canyon where we often used to play. (After having seen other parts of the world I can truly appreciate why people call the Willamette Valley God's Country.)

God blessed me with some good rides, and I made it to the Abbey just as it was getting dark.

CHAPTER 6 - HOW GOD SHOWED THE VANITY OF CEREMONY

It was spring of 1979 at the Trappist Abbey Our Lady of Guadalupe. I had been trying to enter this monastery for two years. Fr. Timothy advised Abbot Bernard that the leadership needed to make a decision as to whether they will accept or refuse me as a monk. To continue stringing me along was to encourage me in a wrong way. The Abbot came and asked me what I thought of the change in the ceremony of the mass. I said I hadn't noticed the change. He told me there had only been a small change. I told him, I hadn't much confidence in ceremony. (I didn't say this to him, but my thought was that ceremony had nothing to do with my born-again experience.) He said, "Well we'll have to get you some books and teach you about these things, and then he left.

Later in the day he came back, and sadly told me a decision was made, and that I would not be accepted into the Abbey. He and the brothers felt I would not fit in because I did not believe in the ceremony and it was very central to the Trappist way. He left. I felt broken-hearted as though I had just been rejected by a sweetheart.

Then I prayed, "God weren't you calling me to this monastery?" Then, for the first time in my life, the thought came to me to open my Bible at random seeking a message from God.

First, I prayed. Then I opened my Bible at random with my eyes closed. In my mind's eye, I saw four columns. One of the columns had a part that was shadowed. I then opened my eyes and read in the area that was shadowed in my Bible. I read, "He that killeth an ox is as if he slew a man; he that sacrifice a lamb, as if he cut off a dog's neck; he that offereth an oblation, as if he offered swine's blood; he that burneth incense, as if he blessed an idol. Yeh, they have chosen their own ways, and their soul delighteth in their abominations. I also will choose their delusions and will bring their fears upon them; because when I called, none did answer; and when I spake they did not hear: but they did evil before mine eyes, and chose that in which I delighted not. Hear the word of the LORD, ye that tremble at his word; your brethren that hated you, that cast you out for my name's sake, said, Let the LORD be glorified: but He shall appear to your joy, and they shall be ashamed." Is.66:3-5 KJV.

I did not immediately understand how miraculously appropriate this passage was. Nor did I yet see how much God hates the vain outward show of religion. Even now, this light is slowly growing brighter. I am only now beginning see that God put that passage there so that after I had made a sincere effort to enter the monastery, He could deeply empress upon me how wrong it all is, and how radically and profoundly deceived the whole world is. I recall a dream I had when living in Israel. I was taking care of dumb and disabled children at Saint Vincent de Paul near Jerusalem.
In the dream, I was in a couch traveling very fast. It was pouring down rain with thunder and lightning.

The drivers of the couch were all wearing shiny black

fisher coats. They were driving me to my wedding. Whipping the black horses to drive them on faster. I was alone in the couch looking out of the couch window hoping that my bride would be beautiful. The drivers were laughing joyously and they were the needy children that I was supposedly taking care of! I recall two of their names, Amir and Ido. Jesus said, "The poor you have with you always." This may take some thought, but the poor and needy are our ticks home.

CHAPTER 7 – GOD'S DELIVERANCE FROM FORMAL EDUCATION

On March 3, 1980 I was studying a religious tract on the Holy Spirit written by Bill Bright, a well known evangelist. I was doing this study in one of the quieter lunch rooms at Portland State University. I was in my senior year working toward a Bachelor's degree in business management. This tract made a reference to John 3:16, but when I looked it up I mistakenly read John 2:16 which says: "And said unto them that sold doves, Take these things hence; make not my father's house an house of business." Suddenly I felt a strong sense of God's presence.

I felt God was telling me to give up studying business. I became deeply entranced. I gathered up my books and slowly but resolutely walked to my next class to inform the professor that I was withdrawing from the University. Then I felt prompted to purchase a journal to record the details of my new walk with the Lord. When I turnd to the third of March I noticed that it said on the top of the page, "The Fast of Esther".

Since fasting was so instrumental in my conversion it had become a very important watch word for me. But I knew nothing yet about the book of Esther, but I would soon become intensely interested in the book of Esther. In retrospect I see that it is a powerful story of how God effects deliverance through godly leaders and united prayer and fasting.

A short time later I was reading the testimony of Ellen G. White and I learned that the Holy Spirit had spoken to her through the book of Esther also. When she asked her spiritual director what it might mean when God spoke to her through the book of Esther, he said that it meant that God had a special call on her life.

CHAPTER 8 - THE PSALM 91 EPIPHANY

I was challenged to seek more and more of God out in the wilderness, I decided to go camping in a forested area in California near the town of Big Sir.

I was camped under a giant Redwood tree. After being there for some time, a man and his son arrived at the same spot. Since I felt God wanted me to be in solitude, I stayed in my tent. I overheard the boy say to his dad, "I wonder where the person is who has that tent." I was extra quiet and prayed that I would not be discovered in my tent.

As it got dark, they pitched their tent. I overheard the dad say that he thought the place was kind of spooky. By morning, the boy and his father packed up their things and left. I was relieved to be alone again.

After a few more days of solitude, it started raining and grew cold so I started praying for sunshine and warmth. Day after day, it just kept raining. I prayed, "Oh God, if the constant rain doesn't stop, I am going back to town." I then went to sleep.

I awakened to rain, so I packed up my gear and started hiking out. Low and behold, as soon as I got out from under the giant Redwood tree, the rain stopped and everything was dry. As I looked back at the tree, I saw that the very tall Redwood trees were catching the fog and causing the constant rain! I realized I could have simply moved out from under the tall Redwood tree and I would have been dry and warmer. But my resolve to persevere in the wilderness had been broken, so I continued to hike out of the forest.

When I got out to the road to hitch hike, the first car that came by gave me a ride. It was two teenage girls, so I got in the back seat. Listening to their conversation, I realized why they picked me up and I got nervous. I wanted these young women to know I was not a partier, so I began to talk very fast telling them my born again experience which caused them to change their tune. They dropped me off at   Interstate 5.

I began to hitch hike North on Interstate 5 to Portland. This time a young man who worked in a Las Vegas casino picked me up. What happened next must remain a secret lest I tempt someone to try something very dangerous. Let me just say I was going toward God. Then suddenly going very fast away from God and unwittingly tempting God! As we drove along, suddenly sounds became very loud and the thought came to me, "I must be still or I will die" I repeated the thought aloud, "I must be still or I will die."

I became alarmed and then I saw a hospital sign, and I asked him to take me to the hospital. He said, "You will be alright." I tried to explain to him why I might be in danger but I could not get him to understand. The thought came to me, "This is a near death experience to teach you to repent. You are not going to die." The thought came to me again, I must be still or I will die." The young man took an interchange that put us on the highway 152 to Salinas CA. The young man dropped me off on the side of highway.

I knew I needed to remain calm so I sat down on the side of the highway because the thought kept coming to me, that I had to trust God more than ever. Then I opened my Bible at random, hoping God would give me a reassuring message. I read, "Declare ye in Judah, and publish in Jerusalem; and say, Blow ye the trumpet in the land: cry, gather together, and say, assemble yourselves, and let us go into the defensed cities" Jer.4:5 KJV I didn't understand what this meant, but my subconscious knew to prepare for war!

As cars kept whipping past me, I just knelt there on the side of the highway with my eyes closed. In my mind's eye I saw a suit of armor and a lance coming toward me. The closer it got to me the more fearful I became so I said aloud, "Get back in the name of Jesus Christ." It would move back and my fear decreased but then the armor and lance started coming toward me again and my fear would increase. Again, I said, "Get back in the name of Jesus Christ." It would move back causing my fear to subside. This continued for some time until the armor and lance stopped coming at me, and then I calmed down and felt better.

I felt a sensation on my forehead between my eyes. The thought came to me to touch my forehead to the ground. As soon as I did, I saw in my mind's eye a huge transparent gold colored hand came out of the sky with the index and middle fingers extended. Under the index finger was my sister Patricia who, was recently widowed, and her son, Mark, was under the middle finger who was now of course fatherless. Then a huge thundering voice said, "LOVEST THOU THESE." I said through tearful eyes, "Yes!" But, I felt like I did not love them enough.

(I learned later, while all this was happening to me, the State of Oregon was trying to take her son from her. After she lost her husband, she had a nervous break- down. The State of Oregon then considered her an unfit mother.)

Then I heard, in my mind's ear, a man's voice say, "John, you have only one reason to live, and that is to preach repentance and the forgiveness of sins in the name of Jesus Christ."

I said, "But what do I say?" I wanted a specific message.

I didn't hear a voice again but the thought came to me, *to pay attention.*

Then I saw a vision of a hovering eagle and from both sides of the eagle came two halves of an encircling bronze shield that crashed together in front of the eagle's breast. Diagonally across the shield in base relief was the capital letters of the word, "**FAITH**".

Initially, I thought of Isaiah 40:31, but many years later, I found an inset study note on the word "hen" while reading the New King James Study Bible, published by Nelson Publishing and edited by the leadership at Western Seminary in Portland, Oregon. This study note on Matthew 23:37 is a miracle to me because in it there are nine references including a reference to Psalms 91:4. This verse matches the above vision perfectly! It reads, "He shall cover thee with his feathers, and under his wings shalt thou trust: his truth shall be thy shield and buckler." Ps. 91:4 KJV

Many years after I had the above vision, God has the leadership at Western Seminary put this study note in their Study Bible! There would be even more years before I would discover it. There are eight more passages, that speak of taking refuge under God's wings. Thy are: (Deut. 32:10-12; Ruth 2:12: Ps. 17:8; 36:7; 61:4; 63:7; Is.31:5; Mal. 4:2). The references speak of God's protective wings, under whose shelter the frightened can find refuge.

Another Bible passage that comes to mind is where Paul writes, "Above all, taking the shield of faith, wherewith ye shall be able to quench all the fiery darts of the wicked." Ephesians 6:16 KJV

CHAPTER 9 - PILGRIMAGE TO ISRAEL

November 1985 I began to get the feeling that I should go to Israel and study Hebrew in order to study the Bible in its original language. I had joined a very radical group of Christians, a group that did not even have a name, technically speaking. They referred to themselves as "the church" and "the brothers". The leader of this group was very secretive and although I had asked him, he refused to tell me his name or testimony.

He was referred to, by the other brothers, as the Elder or Brother Evangelist. I heard him give a message once when he spoke kindly of snakes. At another time, one of the brothers spoke of snake handling but only touched on the subject. It was this radical group, called the brothers that got me interested in learning to speak Hebrew because most of them were studying it.

The brothers also believed that the world was nearing the time of her history when the Jews would accept the gospel of Jesus Christ. I also recalled that I had talked with a Jewish girl on a Greyhound bus back in about 1978. She spoke of Israel and about how there were many young people going there to volunteer to work on the Kibbutzim. I thought, perhaps that is what I should do, especially since I wanted to learn Hebrew.

Before leaving the Brothers and the United States for Israel, I received a miraculous message from the Holy Spirit. I remember the exact date because I had my daily reading marked in my Bible and still have that Bible to this day. It was

November 25, 1985. I do not recall the brother's name, but he seemed to take a disliking to me and at one point said that even, Sarah called Abraham lord, using this fact of scripture to justify his lording it over me. We went to bed and that night I had a dream.

In the dream, I was herding sheep. My sheep were on the water and another shepherd was waiting for me to get my sheep off the water so he could let his sheep on the water. Suddenly this shepherd becomes impatient and begins to shout and wave his arms. This spooked my sheep and some of them pile up against the sheep next to a cliff. The sheep next to the cliff fell to their death.

I did not know what to make of this dream until I read my reading for that day. I know it was on November 25 because I had it marked and I still have this Bible. The passage is Ezekiel 34. When I read it, I understood the dream. God is trying to warn me that I must expect this kind of treatment from the so-called official types who like power and want to lord it over others.

I still had about $400 in a bank account from my last job. When I arrived in New York, I sent for the money. In the meantime, I was homeless and penniless in New York City. It was one of the most stressful periods of my life. I soon learned the ropes though and in the two weeks it took to get my $400, I became accustomed to writing out to suburban churches that gave to shelter the homeless. I remember the news of the space shuttle Challenger exploding only a short while after tack-off. I also recall how in New York, there was China town where

57

everyone spoke Chinese. When I went to the Hispanic part of town and everyone spoke Spanish. It was like being in a foreign country!

The day finally came for me to fly People's express from the Newark New Jersey Airport. I landed in Brussels Belgium February 12, 1986. This was my very first experience of Europe. The city of Brussels near Cologne Germany is enchantingly beautiful especially when you are nearly broke, lost, and do not know anyone or even how to speak the language. It is truly an enchanting feeling! And therefore deserves a little describing. But how do I describe it? Being in a strange faraway country is half of it, but the other half has to do with not knowing where you are going to sleep, or how you are going to eat.

I was completely disoriented and had little or no money. So I was walking by faith, wondering how God will meet my needs. What I have learned is if I trust God, he will put it in the hearts of people to help. However, first I learned I must be trusting enough to put myself at the mercy of God and others. Then I watched and beheld how God puts it into the hearts of others to help.

I went to a place that was romantic which is also part of the equation. There was mist in the air and everything was green. The air was cool. It's beautiful there during the fall, winter and early spring.

By hitchhiking, I finally arrived in southern Italy. Some Italian men gave me a ride to the Naples railroad station where I took the train to catch a boat to Greece.

Sometimes people would invite me to sleep overnight and other times, I slept on the side of the road in a field.

On the ferry to Greece, I met a jet pilot from Turkey. He flew for the Turkish Air Force. He told me he had been in Rome studying communism and recommended I study communism. His contact was to flag him down along the highway. When he got into the car I had to get in the back and I could tell that he didn't like me. He was shifty eyed and acted very ill at ease. They dumped me in the middle of Athens.

I started asking people if they spoke English, and in a little while I found a person who could speak English and pointed me in the direction of the train station. Not knowing that there was an inexpensive hotel nearby, I slept in the train station my first night in Greece.

A couple of runners came by early in the morning and escorted me to a hotel a few blocks away.

Stories of people being turned back at the Israeli port of entry in Haifa for not having enough money began to concern me because I only had about $40 left. I decided to call a family member long distance for a loan of emergency funds so I'd be able to continue on to Israel and have enough money to get through passport control.

When I got him on the phone and told him of my circumstances and plans for Israel, I felt better knowing he would send funds before my money ran out. However, after about 10 days of waiting with no wire for me, I began to wonder and be concerned. Therefore, I called my brother back and he spoke in a very metallic tone of voice the words, "My wife said you got yourself to Greece, so you should be able to get yourself back."

This was very shocking news. I had been wasting time waiting for a money wire that was not even coming! What I hadn't realized was that although I had reconciled with mom and dad over a past problem, I'd overlooked my need to reconcile with my brother and his wife. It's so hard to express deep feelings of hurt and abandonment along with the feelings of rejection.

The feelings of loneliness and insecurity compounded by being alone and broke in a foreign and faraway land where I didn't have any friends and didn't even know the language. My family's rejection of me seemed all the more harsh and cold-blooded when I thought about their own Christian confession. What was I going to do now? A Scripture passage continued to go around and around in my head which was, "Trust ye not in a friend, put ye not confidence in a guide:" Micah 7:5

Within the week, I found some black farm labor in Corinth. A lady from Tara Farm introduced me to a dairy farmer in Solomos about 7 km south of Corinth. Solomos is just 1 km from the ruins of ancient Corinth where St. Paul preached the gospel and established one of the first churches of early Christianity.

60

The South of Greece with its Cyprus trees is one of the most scenic and enchanting places in the world but it must be visited in the winter or spring while the mist is in the air and before hot weather turns the grass brown.

The dairy farmer was in his mid -seventies and could do the work of a young man. He and his wife were very good to me. They treated me like their own son. The farmer taught me some Greek, and his granddaughter also tried to teach me some Greek, but I never learned very much since I'm such a slow learner. I never quite mastered English. After working for him about four months, I got the idea to smuggle leather knitted blouses into Greece from Turkey and sell them to tourist in the streets of Athens.

By going to Istanbul every two weeks, I tripled my money in a month, giving me enough to live and travel on. On my third trip to Istanbul, I left my luggage at the hostel where I checked in and then left to purchase more leather knitted blouses. When I got back to the hostel, I went to get my backpack and could not find it! I asked the people working there if they knew anything about it but they did not. I thought about what valuables I had in it which were a $200 down sleeping bag, a $155 high-tech Kelty backpack, and $120 high tech tent. I also had clothing, my Bible, my birth certificate, and an old US passport!

I soon learned that I was not the only victim. Two English people had also had their backpacks stolen. Whoever stole their backpacks knew what they were doing because these English people also had high-tech equipment plus some very expensive cameras and accessories. They had their things insured.

So we went to the police together and made a report. The next day we had an appointment with the chief of police. He reprimanded the hostel manager and told him he was arresting his employees and closing the hostel. The manager began to weep. I felt sorry for him because I could tell the police chief wanted some excuse to put the manager out of business and now he had one.

That day, I realized why high-tech backpacks were in such high demand. When I shopped around for another high-tech backpack I realized there was none to be had in all of Istanbul or even in Athens! I couldn't believe it! These cities are two of the largest industrial cities in their part of the world and I was told I would not be able to find high-tech recreation equipment at all! Nor could I find a place to buy a Bible! Istanbul Turkey is 98% Muslim.

I purchased some cheap Turkish luggage and put my knitted leather blouses in the new luggage not realizing the Turkish luggage would draw unwanted attention to me. When I arrived at the frontier, a customs officer asked who the luggage belonged to. I said it was mine. He told me to open it. What happened in the next few minutes surprised me a little. When the custom officers saw the leather knitted blouses, he asked me if they were all leather.

I told him yes. He told me to come with him into their offices. I had been told that customs would not do much if I were caught smuggling knitted leather blouses because I was a tourist. But they sealed my bags, and wrote in my passport that I had to leave Turkey with the leather knitted blouses. Then they told me if I broke the seals and sold the leather blouses in Greece, I would be in trouble for smuggling.

I began to get the feeling that it was time to continue on to Israel. I went to the head customs office and talked to a lawyer about getting permission to import the leather into Greece, but it would be expensive and take months. I tried to find out what kind of market for leather blouses I could find in Israel. No one seemed to know for sure. Some of the competition felt that the market in Israel would be good because Israel has a big tourist business.

I figured that the worst thing they would do to a tourist who didn't have any cash, but had $800 plus in merchandise would be to turn me back to Greece. If that happened, then I would take the leather blouses to Italy. The thing that made all this profitable was the very low price of leather in Istanbul and the very inexpensive transport in Greece.

The way my mind rationalized smuggling and not paying customs was that I saw trade tariffs and custom taxes as a greedy way to keep the wealthy wealthy and the poor poor. On this subject I could write a whole book but not here.

So a few days later, I am on the ferry now entering the port of Haifa Israel I was impressed by the beautiful emerald green of the hills surrounding Haifa. But I'm getting more nervous by the minute. A passport control officer asked me for my boarding pass. I could not find my boarding pass! So I went back to the ship to look for it. I couldn't find it and started thinking I was now going to draw unwanted attention to myself at passport control and customs. This put me in near panic, but something in me kept telling me not to panic and stay calm.

I went to the office and told them I lost my boarding pass. They asked me what my number was. I told them and they asked me if I was sure it was my number…I said yes. Then they simply wrote me another boarding pass! By this time I'd been in suspense so long that I couldn't bear the tension any longer and didn't hardly care what happened just as long as it was over with. I was the last one through passport control. I had made up my mind what to do….

I was going to pray and then make a beeline for the exit on the other side of customs without putting my luggage down on customs tables. I had my passport in one hand and walked slowly across the room toward the door expecting a customs officer to stop me at any second. Not even the guard at the door seemed to notice me. I was somehow made invisible. This timing of being last instead of drawing attention to myself, seemed to have the opposite effect! Those who are last are truly first. Hallelujah!

I was so happy to be in Israel. It was all so interesting. I wanted to go where the tourists would be so I could find a market and if I had figured correctly, it would be Jerusalem. I only had enough money to purchase a bus ticket to Jerusalem. The money I had left was not enough to buy a meal much less a place to stay. So, it was about noon when I reached Jerusalem.

I thought if I'm going to have enough money for a place to stay that night, I would have to sell at least one leather blouse. I had to find the market first. I asked which way was town or the market. The thing that struck me first about Israel was how crowded the bus stations were. The next thing was how many people especially young people, could speak   English. It was never difficult to find someone who could speak English.

So I carried about 40 pounds of leather knitted blouses, plus my personal things down to the Jaffa Road to the nearest market. I learned later that the market is called Mehakina Yahuda. It is the largest market for local Jews and not a tourist place.

Not knowing this yet, I found a place on the sidewalk where I saw street vendors. I started putting my leathers out on my tent. One of the vendors who apparently didn't like my looks, started giving me a bad time, obviously trying to run me off. When he realized I didn't speak a word of Hebrew and he couldn't speak any English, he began to resort to things like pinching me!

 Some ladies came up asking about the leather blouses, but I didn't understand a word. I told them by writing on a piece of paper that the price was 15 shekels. I knew I was selling cheap but I was desperate to make a quick sale so I could get settled and oriented.

All of a sudden there was a whole mob of women yelling and pulling at the blouses. All the commotion caught the attention of the shopkeeper nearby. When he saw the low price I was selling at, he knew I didn't know what I was doing and offered to buy all of my leathers for 200 shekels. I was afraid the Israeli women were going to pull on the blouses so hard that the fragile knitting was going to unravel.

The shopkeeper offered to help me by taking my leathers off the street and into his shop. This made the women hysterical. They began to scream and storm the door of the shop. I could not understand what was going on with the women. A policeman came, but he could not speak English either and so the women refused to leave the shop.

Finally, an Orthodox Jew came up who could speak English. He told me why the women were so hysterical. It was because they were afraid the shopkeeper, who had a bad reputation for cheating people, was going to give me a bad price for the leathers and they also wanted a chance to make one more purchase for themselves.

These women yelled and screamed so much that I gave in and sold one or two more blouses at a little less than 15 shekels a piece. Another nearby shopkeeper shouted over in a sarcastic tone, "Are you going to give me one too?" A day or so later, I realized that I could have easily sold them for 45 to 65 shekels.

With a little patience, I could have gotten even a better price than that because my product was exclusive. When I finally sold the last one, it was coming unraveled. I was not going to sell it, but one Israeli woman was so bent on having it, in spite of the condition it was in, I sold it to her at a reduced price. I soon learn I'm a year or two too old to work on a Kibbutz or a Moshav which required people to be 35 years or younger. I wondered what I was going to do for a living. Having studied business, I understood that if I was going to make a living street vending then I had to invest capital into some inventory quickly. I chose to invest in jewelry.

Within a short time of selling my new product, I became settled and decided to register in a Hebrew language program called an Ulpan. To improve my learning ability I started a strict diet of the healthiest food and stopped eating all junk foods and desserts. After a few weeks on this diet a curious thing happened. I started thinking about my devotional life and relationship with God.

HOW THE LORD INTIMATES TO JOHN TO GIVE UP THE JEWLLERY BUSINESS

One day as I was browsing through a used bookshop in Jerusalem, I happened across a small book with an interesting cover and title. On the cover was a painted giant pilgrim with a big beautiful walking stick. He was taking giant strides down a footpath that winded its way into an enchantingly beautiful setting. This giant pilgrim was curiously followed by a multitude of people. The title of this small but intriguing book was *The Journey to the East*, and the author was none other than Herman Hesse. I read this book that night and it had a very curious impact on me.

My conscience began to pain me because I was spending all my time buying and selling and my spiritual life was dying. I finished *The Journey to the East* late that night and since it was now Sabbath, I stayed home to pray and fast. On the first day of the week I read *The Journey to the East* a second time. I felt God was telling me He wanted me to quit selling jewelry and to return to my home in America. I also felt He wanted me to go to the small church in Jerusalem, which I had recently heard about. I did not know what would happen there. I did not know exactly where was going, having not been in the southeast part of Jerusalem before. But having received good directions from Jim and Leslie Schultz I found the small church.

I realized immediately that it was a Pentecostal group because people were speaking in tongues. A man gave a short message about how we should all join in and praise God together. A very profound subject, but the speakers anointing or ability did not seem equal to the subject. The man disappeared altogether and a woman in a red dress led the meeting from that point on. She asked if there was anyone needing prayer, to come up for the laying on of hands.

At the beginning, I felt the Lord stirring my heart to go up and ask for prayer to be delivered from my obsession for selling jewelry. Other people went up. One by one, almost everyone there went up to the front for prayer. It looked like the customary thing to do so I finally went up as well.

The prayer went on for a better part of an hour and the woman in the red dress was still calling people to come forward for prayer. If my recollection was correct, there was only one person in a whole group that didn't go up for prayer. That person's name shall remain anonymous. The woman leading the prayer asked why I wanted prayer. I told her I felt God telling me to pray for deliverance from the jewelry business.

She asked, "Are you sure God is telling you to give this jewelry business up? I said yes, all the while noticing the women who was leading the whole thing was covered in jewelry. Yet, I believed that God could deliver me in spite of her if there were at least one other true believer present. I left that meeting never to return because of that woman's overbearing leadership role. Notwithstanding, I never sold jewelry again after that night of prayer. Praise be to God! Hallelujah!

In October of 1987 I sold the jewelry business to a jewelry store in Eilat. I was looking for a month extension on my visa by crossing the frontier into Siani. My visa expired that very day and there was no bus on the Egyptian side till 10 AM the next morning. So I decided to hike to my favorite spot in the foothills near the border checkpoint.

I didn't figure it would matter if my visa had expired by just a few hours. But when I went down to pass through passport control, the woman in charge told me I would now have to go back to Eilat to the ministry of the Interior and pay $20 and get an exit visa. I thought to myself, if I have to pay $20, I might as well try to get a regular three-month extension to my visa, and if they will not do that, then I'll ask for an exit visa.

Hallelujah! I received a regular three month extension on my visa. What a pleasant surprise!

Now I could return to Jerusalem. I applied for a position at St. Vincent D` Paul, a home for severely handicapped children. It is located in a Jerusalem suburb called Ain Kerem. This is a very beautiful area in the traditional site of St. John the Baptist's home. The Church of the Visitation is here. A very beautiful church building. About 5 km to the west into the wilderness, there lies a monastery called St. John of the desert.

Now days, there are quite a lot of pine trees in this area. About 30 or 40 year-old trees. About hundred meters further west, lies a Protestant cloister for three nuns where I used to go for retreats. This cloister is called St. Elizabeth because the chapel is built over the traditional site of St. Elizabeth's grave.

On October 30, 1987 I moved into a private room and bath that would be my home for nearly 2 years. This is difficult to write about because it's a period of my life that I'm ashamed of. I've just arrived at St. Vincent's and I'm in the cafeteria, when a girl accosts me and introduces herself. Her name was Bella and she was from Germany. In the days following she sat regularly at the English-speaking table and I could tell she liked me. She was only 19 then. Very intelligent, but slightly overweight and this perhaps is why I didn't care for her at first. Nevertheless, she continued to be very friendly with me and offered to give me free lessons in the French language. I accepted the offer and we spent all of our free time together.

One morning, I awoke with the thought that I needed to make a decision about how serious I was going to get about Bella. I was afraid she was going to get hurt. That morning, I decided to look for things I liked about Bella so I could make a decision as to whether or not I should encourage her.

She had lost weight because of a brief illness, and one morning during a French lesson I was attracted to her eyes. As we were talking, I looked deeply into her eyes in the morning sunlight and noticed that her eyes were unusually beautiful turquoise and green color. I told her that her eyes were beautiful.

After that morning, I fell deeply in love with Bella. One evening we went for a walk into a park a couple of miles away. We sat on a bench and I shared my testimony with her about how I came to be a born-again Christian.

On another evening, we went for a walk and it was on this walk that I had plans to tell her I was in love with her. We walked into the village of Ain Kerem looking for an out-of-the-way place to talk and embrace. I told her that I did not believe in sex or kissing before marriage. I told her that I liked her.

She asked, "What do you mean?"

I said, "I mean I'm interested in you as a woman."

Then this deep moan or sigh escaped her. And she said she was not a woman but a girl of only 19 years of age and that marriage was something she did not want for at least five years!

This was very painful news to me.

Earlier, I had wanted to embrace her and hold her in my arms, now it seemed inappropriate. I looked up and noticed a silhouette of a grove of Cyprus against the night sky. I felt extreme inner pain and was disappointed. With a big sigh I said, "This is the most difficult time of the year for me." I then became aware that there was a full moon, it was nearing my birthday, and it was fall, my favorite time of year.

Bella misunderstand what I meant but I never bothered to explain to her that I always felt more tempted around the time of a full moon and around the time of my birthday. It seemed that I was forever falling in love at this time of the year. These influences are subtle yet powerful. Only those with heightened levels of intuition become more aware of these influences.

I had become interested in reading, *Faust* by Geothe. When Bella heard this, she became excited because it was a favorite of hers as well. We read the end of part one together. Bella informed me she would be leaving Israel early in January to return to school in Germany.

This too, I found painful. I tried to talk her out of it. Her mother was a tax accountant and she was very much under her mother's influence. Bella hated her only brother, but was devoted to her mother and seemed indifferent toward her father. The women seemed to dominate the household. I tried desperately to share my faith with Bella.

About this time, I had a dream. There was a windstorm and rioting in the streets of Jerusalem. People were putting their shutters up for protection. I did not have shutters for my house and I was wearing a T-shirt. I felt very vulnerable. I went into my house and then I heard a loud knocking at the door.

I became apprehensive but opened the door to find Bella in the custody of two men dressed half like priests and half like policemen. Bella looks like she didn't want me to show that I knew her and shame was written on her face with her head bowed. I asked what they wanted, but they then left abruptly without saying a word. I had the feeling that I should rescue Bella. At first, I did not recognize the men, but later I recognized them as being the son and son-in-law of the pastor of an English Pentecostal church that we had been attending.

Shortly after the dream, I realize Bella was under tremendous social pressure from her peers. The German Society is a very proper and legalistic society and Bella is becoming troubled with the responsibility of our relationship and the great difference in our ages. The age difference was not what bothered me the most, it was my resolve to remain single and chased for the kingdom of heaven that caused me the most concern. It seemed that our relationship was doomed even from its very inception.

To make things worse, one day Bella asked me, "How do you know the devil really exists?"

I answered her, "For me the question is not whether the devil exists, but where is he now?"

Instantly, she hid her face. I sat waiting for her to see how long it would take her to regain her composer.

There was a wall of ice between us. Finally, after what seemed like a long time, I began to sense her plight and began to feel compassion. I felt I should try to break the ice.

Gradually, we resumed our conversation. A few days later, I began to see a change in Bella. She was withdrawing and became very cold. At the same time, I felt the need to tell her about my private resolution to remain celibate. Finally, one day we went for a walk and I told her. I asked her what had happened to our relationship.

She would not tell me, but one day she admitted that something had happened and she was gradually becoming aware of a great difference between us. I wondered what it was. I racked my brain trying to figure out what happened. First, I thought it was when I told her about my resolve to remain celibate. Much later, it finally dawned on me that the beginning of the end of our relationship was the day she asked how I knew the devil really existed and hid her face.

The date of her departure in January came and Bella left for Germany. I knew I would never see her again and the feelings of loss, loneliness, and grief were the most intense of my life. We corresponded, but her letters gave me no hope. I felt like someone drowning. Even before she left, I had found myself spending hours in different area churches weeping. The feeling with Bella was a sense of mutual love that was very deep but it was not really mutual.

Perhaps, I wept because I had a glance or a taste of how sweet a deepened mutual love could be. Or perhaps, it was because I knew deep inside this love would never be consummated. One day, I told her I preferred being alone with my thoughts of her rather than being in a crowd with her.

If I could not be alone with her, I preferred being alone with my thoughts of her. More than once, she said that I seemed to love her too much. I began to suspect this myself and wondered if my love for her was idolatrous. One day at church services I prayed and asked God if there was anything displeasing in my life. And in my mind's eye I saw the face of Bella! I then resolved to break off my relationship with Bella completely. Shortly after, I burned all her letters to me, her photos, and blotted out her address in my address book.

I had been reading other renditions of *Foust* and also read the legend that was the source. The true story was not so romantic as Geothes' *Foust*. Indeed, it was a terrible story about how he sold his soul to the devil for 12 years of pleasure and some supernatural power.

At the end of the 12 years, the devil came for the man and tore his body to pieces. I realized that Geothe had only romanticized the gruesome truth. I remembered then that Bella seemed convinced that he was not a Christian and had a very definite connection to the occult.

75

About this time, the idea to start a morning prayer meeting came to me. A small group of us began to pray at 5:30 am every morning. After reading a book entitled Risky Living by Jamie Buckingham I felt prompted to begin using my prayer tongue which was a gift the Holy Spirit had given to me years ago just six months after my conversion experience.

I started praying in tongues regularly and my terrible feeling of loss and grief for Bella left me. I had joy in my heart and a desire to shout and sang praises to God! As the prayer meeting grew my knowledge of the importance of forgiveness and the reality of demons was also growing. One of the men in the group asked for prayer for deliverance from a particular demon in his life.

I counseled him to begin fasting before we did the exorcism. I commanded the demons come out of him in the name of Jesus Christ. I told the man to take a deep breath and breathe out hard while also commanding the demons come out of himself. The man began to hiss and fell out of the chair to the floor frothing and convulsing slightly. After this the man said he was experiencing a new feeling of joy and freedom to praise God. Hallelujah! We were careful to thank God for this man's deliverance.

Others began to seek me out for prayer. God seem to be answering every prayer. We continued in faithfulness and love for God which made us very joyful. Sometimes I was so joyful I could not sleep. One day I felt an anointing come on be so strong that I wept. I felt prompted to witness to a certain member of the community who was a Muslim who had previously asked for prayer.

I shared a little of my faith and testimony but sensed the door was firmly closed. Yet another person who was overhearing our conversation came to me later and asked for prayer and the laying on of hands so he could receive the gift of Holy Spirit. I agreed to pray for him if he would agree to confess his sins and read some Bible passages referring to the gift of the Holy Spirit.

About a week later he confessed his sins so our prayer group prayed for him with the laying on of hands and also baptized him by complete immersion in water at a swimming pool. He received the gift of tongues a short time later.

At St. Vincent's, we were having three different prayer meetings which were growing. The pastor was giving anointed messages about how the devil hated and envied David and how King Saul also began to hate and envy David. During this message a woman slid out of her chair moaning and screaming as her body convulsed on the floor. The pastor discerned this as a manifestation of an unclean spirit and began shouting and commanding the evil spirits come out of her in name of Jesus Christ. The prayer meeting turned into absolute pandemonium.

About two thirds of the group seemed to be fearful while the others drew closer and shouted at the unclean spirit to come out in the name of Jesus Christ. Finally the girl lay still and unconscious. She became conscious again a few minutes later and some of her friends took her to her room. Our prayer group rejoiced and gave thanks to God.

The Saint Vincent de Paul leadership called for a large prayer meeting all volunteers and employees were expected to attend and I was scheduled to say the closing prayer. I stood up and said," Thank you Lord that you are present here now in the sweet love of your Holy Spirit."

Just at that point many people began to cough cutting my prayer short.

In the crowd I noticed the Muslim that I had tried to share my faith with earlier whom I had sensed a firmly closed door with. She was coughing uncontrollably like an automatic rifle and suddenly ran out of the building. I told my friend, Shalom, that I thought she needed help, so we went outside to find her. We found her in the parking lot still coughing in a very strange way. I asked her if I could lay hands on her and pray for her. She knotted yes, so I began to pray in tongues over her and she recovered immediately. A few onlookers began to slander our prayer group so we began a special secret prayer project for these onlookers. We prayed that the spirit of God would bring conviction upon them. The result was most dramatic. They attended our prayer group intending to disrupt and verbally attack us. They insisted that they bring their dog to the prayer meetings. We told them the dog could not attend so they decided to never come back. Praise the Lord.

In January of 1989 during my morning devotions, I asked the LORD what the signs of the end times were. Three visions flashed across my mind. First, I saw Jews returning to Israel, second I saw the formation of the European Economic Community, and thirdly I saw Christian revival in Africa and Asia. That same day an acquaintance dropped by to chat which turned into the acquaintance scoffing me when I told him that in my vision I saw a trickle of Jews turn into a large river of Jews coming to Israel out of Russia. He scoffed and said that Israel becoming a state and the new Russian revolution was just something man was doing.

The Holy Spirit revealed to me a passage of Scripture that I had never quite understood. For the first time I realized that it referred to the Temple Mount in Jerusalem. I understood it better because I was living in Israel and had walked on the Temple Mount and had studied its sacred history. This place was where Abraham had prepared to sacrifice Isaac, and where King David built an altar and did sacrifice to stay the plague.

The Holy Spirit brought to my memory Matthew 24:15 where Jesus says, "When ye therefore shall see the abomination of desolation, spoken of by Daniel the prophet, stand in the holy place, whosoever readeth, let him understand."

Also Paul wrote, "Let no man deceive you by any means: for that day shall not come, except there come a falling away first, and that man of sin be revealed, the son of perdition; who opposes and exalted himself above all that is called God, or that is worshiped; so that he as God sitteth in the Temple of God, showing himself that he is God." (2Thess. 4:3-4)
On March 30, 1989 the Jerusalem Post had a story on the front page telling of a trickle of Jews becoming a river pouring out

of the Soviet Union. Later I came across Jeremiah 16:14-15. "Therefore, behold, the days come, saith the Lord, that it shall no more be said, the Lord liveth, that brought up the children of Israel out of the land of Egypt; but, the LORD liveth that brought up the children of Israel from the land of the North, and from all the lands whether he had driven them: and I will bring them again into their land that I gave unto their fathers." The events taking place intensely aroused my interest in eschatology so I began to study more prophecy.

On August 2, 1990, the Gulf War broke out in Israel. My friend, Frank and I are camping out in the Qumran Caves. Missiles were being fired at Israel and gas masks were needed. Many of the volunteers helping in ministry decided to flee because of the war. Frank returned to the States, but I remained in Israel. This was a time of disruption in my living situation and in ministry. But my faith in the Lord grew stronger through His holy word. There were times I experienced rejection, loneliness, and lack but God was clearly excepting me, being my friend, and supplying my needs.

My visa was coming to an end and I knew it would be unlawful for me to stay in Israel without papers. I had an offer to return to Greece but it required me to marry the granddaughter of the dairy farmer I had previously worked for. This did tempt me but I did not give in to the devil and remained in **God**'s will as a eunuch. God made this very clear to me through his Scriptures.

Since I did not know where to go, I decided to seek God by casting lots. I wrote down all the places I thought God might be to go on separate pieces of paper and folded them. I prayed to God about this and told him that if I tossed them in the air, I would go to the place of whichever piece of paper fell closest to me. I unfolded the piece of paper that fell nearest me and it said Mount Athos.

I ended up in a monastery but did not like Mount Athos because there was so much pressure to convert to Greek orthodoxy. I was experiencing a lot of persecution for my faith in Christ so I went for a walk to the woods one day to get distance from the monastery. I admitted to God that I was becoming confused.

I was reminded, that the devil is the author of confusion and darkness resides in him who wants to deceive. I resolved that these people had chosen to believe a delusion. My mistake was that I started trusting and listening to men rather than God. When I started doubting the revelations God had been giving me over the years I began to go to blind guides for help. Suddenly I clearly saw there were deceiving spirits in all the places I had sought God with the help of man. I determined never to doubt the revelations God Himself had given to me and stayed my course.

The deception and delusion that inhabit Greek Orthodoxy, the Roman Catholic Church, and the monasteries I was involved in had continually created doubt in the revelations God had given me. I must never again doubt these revelations so I prayed, "O God please help me. Where do I draw the line? Must I go and live in the wilderness alone?"

God worked out my visa problem so I could go to Israel but I was determined not to live underground. I thought of going to Tel Aviv and figured if God wanted me in Israel He would make a way. It was the summer of 1991 when I went back to the ministry of Interior in Jerusalem. My first thought was that I might be making a mistake but I decided to get an extension on my visa so I would have time to establish my Jewish ancestry and make an application to be an Israeli citizen.

The chief immigration officer told me I needed an affidavit from my Rabbi in America that stated my parents are Jewish. I explained I was not raised Jewish and neither were my parents.

I asked, "What does one do when they believe they are Jewish but records were lost generations ago?"

The chief immigration officer shrugged her shoulders and said, "Just convert."

I said, "I'm already converted."

She asked, "What is the name of the Rabbi that converted you?"

I thought Jesus Christ was the Rabbi that converted me but I knew that answer would not do, so I told her the Rabbi that converted me was God.

She replied, "Well, God can't write affidavits."

The conversation was reminding me of what the Greek Orthodox people had previously told me to do to become a Greek citizen and live at Mount Athos. I could not give them lip service because it would cause me to compromise my Christian convictions and violate my conscience. So the next step was to go to the Rabbinic court in Jerusalem. I was interviewed by a Russian Jewess who could speak very good English. I inquired of her how to prove I had Jewish ancestors. She too, said I needed a letter from a Rabbi.

I said, "What do you do when you and all your living relatives were not raised Jewish? Russia must have plenty of such cases since religion there was suppressed for the past 70 years."

She answered, "Well, just hire some witnesses."

I said, "That's dishonest!"

She said, "Well, they do it you know."

I thought to myself. All I have to do is become a hypocrite. Give the Jewish religion lip service, and bingo. I can become an Israeli citizen! Well I am not that desperate. I will not live a lie and be a hypocrite in order to do what I believe is God's will in an insane contradiction. It is unfortunate. Many people living in Israel are living a lie out of desperation.

The chief immigration officer asked me to write a letter stating why I wanted to stay in Israel. I went to the library, being homeless, and wrote the letter.

The next morning during my morning devotions I prayed, and asked GOD to anoint the letter. And therefore asked Him if there was anything he disapproved of in the letter.

He answered, "Yes… You failed to mention my son Jesus!"

I said, "O GOD if I tell them that I believe Jesus is Your Son, they will throw me out of Israel for sure!"

God did not reply. So I wrote the letter over again confessing that I was a believer in Jesus Christ. And since my born-again experience, I had received a super rational affinity for the Jewish people and the State of Israel.

I took the letter to the chief immigration officer. I had to come back every couple of weeks to check if my application to become an Israeli citizen was accepted.

The third time I came back to check on my application the chief immigration officer told me my application was back. But, she also told me it had been rejected and I was ordered to leave Israel immediately!

I explained that I did not have money to travel immediately.

She wanted to know why I did not have a return trip ticket.

I told her I had one but the return trip was to Israel. Then she told me it was my responsibility to make plans to leave Israel immediately.

I told her I needed time to earn money for a ticket to make plans to leave.

She asked me if I was going to work in Israel illegally.

I told her no.

She said I could go.

As I walked down the hall, I realized I should go back and ask her if she could give me an exit visa. So I did and she said, "I will give you an exit visa, but only when you get your return ticket."

On December 5, 1991 I purchased an open ticket from Haifa To Cypress for $55. I took the ticket to the ministry of the Interior. I asked to apply for reentry papers of which they said I would have to go to the Israel Consulate in Cyprus to do that.

I had heard that messianic Jews who believed Jesus was the Messiah and the Son of God were lied to concerning reentry so I was suspicious. Yet I felt very strongly that God did not want me to go back to America. So I left for Cyprus with a friend.

When we got to Cyprus, the immigration officer asked me, "How much money you got?" I answered, "One hundred dollars." He said, "A hundred dollars! Coffee money. You ain't gitten in." Then he asked my friend, Harry Woodly, "How much money you got?" Harry lied, "A hundred dollars." The immigration officer said, "You ain't gitten in either." We are escorted to another room where Harry and I began discussing how we would resolve our predicament. As Harry and I began discussing what we should do the thought occurred to me that the authorities might be listening to us. I looked up, saw two speakers directly overhead. I put my finger to my lips and pointed up at the speakers overhead and we went silent. Then briefly made our plans by whispering.

After about 20 minutes, the immigration officer came with the ships First officer and said that he would be willing to let us stay in Cyprus if we could give him some assurance that we would not stay more than a week. Then he questioned me, "You are a religious person, right?"

I said yes.

Then he said if you give me your word that you will not stay more than a week, then I will let both of you get off the ship.

Then suddenly he changed his mind and said no they are not getting into Cyprus. They were speaking in Greek so I couldn't understand. The immigration officer started pointing his finger at me and ranting in English, "Israel is not going to let this one back in!"

At this point I was extremely tempted to go back to Greece and stay with the dairy farmer who treated me as one of his own sons because I had a round-trip ticket that included free meals. But I felt the main reason I was not allowed to stay in Cyprus was because God wanted me back in Israel. I recalled that I had prayed that God would close the door to Cyprus if I was not to go there and returned to Israel. This is exactly what was happening.

I was concerned that Israel would think that I was being disobedient to their government. When the boat arrived at the port of Haifa I got in line for passport control and Harry decided to go his own separate way to a different passport line. I never saw Harry again but, before we parted ways he gave a generous gift of $150 and we corresponded by letter.

When I got to the front of the line I gave my passport to the woman there. She put my passport number and name into the computer and then she called for her superior. They exchanged a few words in Hebrew that I did not understand then I was escorted to a chair inside where the chief officers were.

I asked an officer what was wrong and why I was not allowed to continue on. He told me that it had been entered into the computer that I was not to be allowed back into Israel because I had previously overstayed my visa.

I waited about an hour until they had finished processing all the new arrivals from the ship. Then with some paperwork and officer escorted me back to the ship. When the captain saw me he exclaimed, "Are you still here?"

I told him what had happened and he asked me what I wanted to do. I told him I wanted to stay in Israel.

He said, "Ok I will fix it."

So I began to feel hopeful. I walked down with the captain to the going plank and when I finished talking with him, a woman police officer asked me if I had papers to get off the ship.

I said, "No".

She ordered, "Then get back up on deck and don't come back down."

I actually thought about jumping overboard swimming under the docks but then I would have to leave my backpack and personal property behind. Not to mention it would probably make things much worse.

Evening began to approach and it was passed the time for the ship to disembark. I went downstairs and waited. Then suddenly a woman police officer approached and asked me if I was John. I answered that I was and stated that I didn't want to be deported. She told me not to worry because no decisions had been made yet. She then inquired about my volunteer work at St. Vincent for handicapped children.

Other police officers joined our conversation with smiles giving me a sense of acceptance because they knew of my work and told me it was good. I thought that God was doing some miracle with immigration officials changing their mind to let me stay in Israel until my legal status could be resolved.

So I ran upstairs to get my backpack and hurried down to get off the ship into a nearby car they had arranged. It was only much later that I realized the significance of the civilian car and all the friendly men all in civilian clothes. The men all seemed unusually friendly as they took me to the port of Haifa police station. We all went inside and waited for a while and one of the police officers brought me a soda.

I asked the woman police officer who had informed me that I had permission to get off the boat why immigration had changed their minds. She no longer had a smiling face and said, "Nothing has changed."

Then an officer came out who I thought might be the chief duty officer speaking something to me in Latin.

He said, "Ha! Persona non grata!"

I told him I have been looking forward to becoming a citizen of Israel. Since he did not have the heart to break the bad news to me himself, he did an about face and went and hid in his office. Leaving it to the clerk to break the bad news to me.

Then a clerk at the desk shoved a form at me and said, "You have been arrested for being in Israel illegally and will be deported at your own expense. (money again) I looked up at the women police officer who had lied to me saying I could get off the ship.

She hid her face pretending to be busy with work on her desk.

I was shocked back into reality and suddenly realized that I had been tricked into leaving the ship. I was outraged. In my heart God was telling me that all things work together for good to those that love the Lord so I calmed myself down and said I wanted to call the US Embassy. They said I could call in the morning and took me to a jail cell to share with an Israeli man named Hiem.

Hiem was in jail for unpaid debt and very depressed because his wife and her divorce attorney had betrayed him and tricked him out of all his millions! In the cell I thought of the book called *Prison to Praise*. It seemed the Holy Spirit wanted me to speak comforting words to this man because he had told me he thought God was angry with him. So I explained that God may be angry with him but that God also loved him and cared for him. I went on to share John 3:16. "For God so loved the world that He gave his only begotten Son, that whosoever would believe in Him should not perish, but have eternal life."

Even though this man was Jewish and did not believe in Jesus Christ I did not lose my confidence to speak what I knew was the truth. As I continued to share the truth from the New Testament, Hiem went to sleep.

In the morning Hiem said, "John, I need to tell you something. Remember when you spoke to me last night? Something strange happened. A wonderful peaceful feeling came over me and I fell asleep, and slept well for the first time in a long time!"

When the man told me this I was delighted. I took it as a confirmation that GOD was pleased and the Holy Spirit was at work. Hallelujah!

My second day in jail, two other men were put in the cell. All they wanted to talk about was getting drunk and chasing whores. I told them that getting drunk and fornication is sin. At first they did not understand the English word fornication. So I began to explain what it meant and they started laughing and talking in Hebrew.

I asked Hiem what the two men were saying in Hebrew. He told me that they were saying a funny feeling comes over them and they started to go to sleep when I spoke to them. Later they were transferred to another cell and I was finally allowed to call the US Embassy in Tel Aviv. The woman I spoke with was a Christian and sounded sympathetic. She said she would contact the US consulate in Haifa and have someone sent to represent me.

The next morning an American came to see me. There was a big problem though. The police had talked to him and had poisoned his mind against me before I ever had a chance to present my case. I overheard a woman police officer talking to him very politely about him having recently becoming an Israeli. He asked me plenty of questions and gave me forms to fill out. He asked me if I wanted my parents to be informed. I told him I could call my brother Allen and that would be sufficient.

Then he started asking me about a missing page of my passport. I explained that it had been stolen and separated along with some of my other luggage when I first arrived to the country.

He mocked me and said. "Come on now, you don't expect me to believe that do you?"

At this point, I was sure this man did not come to help me.

I was tempted to think that the entire cosmos was against me but I recalled I had the truth, and therefore, God was on my side.

So I looked him straight in the eye and said, "Look, I'm telling you the truth, and I can say that with a clear conscience."

This man seemed to already know all about my Christian faith even though I had not said a word about it to him. He said he didn't believe it was honest to follow signs from God. Then he asked me how I got along with my family and why I left America. I was honest and told him my family thought I was crazy to stay in Israel when it was at war with Iraq.

Then he asked, "Do many people think you are crazy?"

I saw what he was leading up to and said, "I hope you know who you are serving."

He said, "I am serving the God of the Jews."

I said, "There is only one God."

He said, "Yea that's what the Jews teach." Implying that Christians teach that there are three gods.

After this I was escorted back to my cell with the realization that it was my Christian faith that was keeping me in jail. Yet, they would not want me or anyone else to know that they are in the business of persecuting Christians.

The next day December 22, 1991, I was taken to court to a district judge. I was constantly tempted to think about what I would say , but Jesus said , "But when they deliver you up, take no thought before hand what ye shall speak, neither do ye premeditate: but whatsoever shall be given you in that hour, that speak ye: for it is not ye that speak, but the Holy Ghost." (Mark 13:11) the Bible directed that the Holy Spirit would tell me what to say when I was put before the judge.

The judge spoke to me in Hebrew. I indicated I spoke in English then, in English, he asked me if I had anything to say.

I told him I didn't know what I was being charged with.

The judge stated I had a history of overstaying my visa.

I said that was a lie and pointed at my passport indicating that all he had to do was look at it to see that I had not overstayed my visa.

He began speaking Hebrew to the secretary court clerk and never once looked at my passport. Then something strange happened. The Judge asked me if I wanted an attorney.

I answered, "Yes I want an attorney"

Then the Judge said, "Did you say God is your attorney?"

I answered, "Yes, God is my attorney."
I asked if I would have the right to appeal and he said in a
mocking tone, "Of course, Israel is a democracy like
America."

Since this Judge was not willing to help, I asked to call for an
attorney from the United States. They let me call an attorney
who said he would take my case to the Supreme Court for
$1400. When I heard that figure, the Holy Spirit reminded me
that Jesus said, "Behold, I send you forth as sheep in the midst
of wolves…" (Matthew 10:16) Then I recalled the advice from
a pastor who said a lawyer will take your money and then you
will be kicked out of the country anyway. So I asked the
attorney from the United States if I could write the letter of
appeal to the Supreme Court myself. He explained that I could,
but it wasn't likely that they would hear the case if it wasn't
drawn up by an attorney.

I wrote a letter anyway, recalling that I had only 48 hours
according to this lawyer. Then I asked the police to let me mail
it, but they said the post office was closed, and that I could do
it in the morning. Later, I learned they had lied to me about
that as well.

The man who was locked up for debt was released, so I was
alone in the cell which gave me time to reflect on how
everyone in jail seemed to be there because they didn't have
money. I thought that had I been rich, I would not have been
put through this whole chain of events because I would have

been able to buy my way out. Then I remembered how the Russian woman at the Rabbinic court in Jerusalem had told me I could hire witnesses to say that I was a Jew.

The next morning I asked for the guard because I wanted to mail my letter of appeal but no one would even come close to my cell. I felt this was a great obstruction of justice.

My letter said, I am appealing the deportation order on the following grounds:
1. The evidence in my passport shows that there has never been a lapse of time between the visa expiration date and the departure date.
2. In 5 1/2 years, I have never received a fine or paid any money for overstaying a visa.
3. The chief immigration officer in Jerusalem always gave me permission to stay till I could acquire money and a ticket to travel out of Israel.
4. The chief immigration officer never gave me any warning that I was in any danger of losing my privilege to visit Israel.
5. The evidence in my file shows that the ministry of the Interior was at least negligent if not deliberate in creating the circumstances leading to my arrest and deportation. I feel confident I can gather evidence to prove police entrapment on the part of the ministry of the Interior if given time and liberty to work on my case.

I feel deeply hurt and wronged, especially since I served Israel for almost two years as a volunteer, and did not flee Israel during the Gulf War. Israel and the God of Israel have first place in my heart. I'm ready to renounce my United States citizenship if necessary. I feel God has given me solemn warnings per Jeremiah 42:18-19 not to return to my life in America.

When the time would come for me to renew my visa, I would always faithfully make application, and then patiently wait for a reply from the head office of the ministry of the Interior. I was made to return many times over a period of months only to be told that my application had been rejected. The last time that I was told, by the immigration officer at Jerusalem, that I had to leave Israel immediately.

I did not have enough money to purchase a ticket, therefore, I asked if I would be given a visa to leave Israel when I bought the ticket and the immigration officer agreed. I also applied for a reentry visa, but was denied this, which the clerk told me to apply at that Israeli Embassy in Cyprus. That I was *persona non grata* was kept secret from me. And I was not warned that it had been entered into their computers to refuse me a reentry into Israel. On the contrary, this information was kept secret from me deliberately.

Before I left my home in Israel, I prayed with my Christian friends that if it was not God's will for me to travel to Cyprus that he would close that door. When I arrived at the Port of Cyprus, the immigration officer denied entry because I did not have enough money. I took this as an answer to my prayers and a sign that God was not willing that I should stay in Cyprus, but wanted me to return to Israel.

When I arrived back at the Haifa Port, Passport Control told me that it had been entered into their computers to refuse me reentry on the grounds that I had overstayed my visa. Papers were made up, and I was escorted back to the ship. I was told by the ship's officers that I could use their radio to call the American Embassy in Cyprus and arrange for an embassy official to intercept me from the immigration office who would not let me enter Cyprus.

However, I was told I could not do this until the ship disembarked from Israel. Then just minutes before the ships departure, a group of Port police came on board the ship and engaged me in friendly conversation up until the time I was told I could leave the ship. This led me to believe that the immigration authorities had changed their minds and were now going to grant me at least a temporary visa, and give me time to sort things out.

However, once I was in the police station and the ship had left everything changed again, and I realized I had been tricked. I was now all of a sudden under arrest for being in Israel illegally, and told I would be deported at my own expense. This I believe, is called police entrapment, and in America, is unlawful. The next day I was rushed before a judge for a mockery of a trial. When I asked the judge if I had the right to appeal, he said I did because Israel was a democracy just like America. However, since I've been arrested I've not been allowed to mail my letter of appeal.

I've never been tricked, wronged, and lied to so often in so short a space of time in all of my life. Is not Israel supposed to be the holy land? The Jewish Bible in Exodus 23:9 says, "Thou shalt not oppress a stranger."

I feel the spirit of God now prompting me to write, "Therefore I will judge you, O house of Israel, everyone according to his way, saith the Lord God. Repent and turn yourselves from all your transgressions; so iniquity will not be your ruin." Ezekiel 18:30.

Sincerely,
Brother John
Cell number 18

On January 8, 1992, I was finally allowed to mail my letter. I don't know if it was ever posted. But I'm getting ahead of myself, the next day if I recall correctly was December 24 Christmas eve. I was transferred to one of Israel's most infamous prisons. I was always put in handcuffs and escorted by an armed guard as though I were a dangerous hardened criminal.

While waiting in front of another jail in Haifa, a young Israeli who looked like a bum came and sat in the paddy wagon with me.

After a short silence, he suddenly blurted out, "You don't believe in fucking?"

I replied, "No."

Then he said, "Man, you must be crazy!"

It appeared that my reputation had caught up with me. This bum had heard the story of how I was fired at a Moshav because I objected to their racketeering in prostitution.

When I was processed into the jail, it was obvious that this too was a trick to rip off more of my valuables. They took notice that I had in my backpack some valuables like a pocket knife and then let me take it with me into the cell. I was put in a cell with six men and six beds. Five of the men were in for theft and one was in for life for murder.

The first thing I did was to share the gospel of Jesus Christ with the whole cell and the man who spoke English the best, translated for those who didn't speak English.

After I shared the gospel with them, they all insisted I take a shower, but when I tried to take a shower, they all descended upon my luggage. So I came out of the shower. Then they said, "you might as well take your shower because we are going to take what we want anyway! So I said, Look it is Christmas so I will let each of you have something. Well it was Christmas, and I had just proclaimed Jesus. I could see how they each coveted their respective gift. I had never seen such intense coveting in my life. They reminded me of children opening their gifts at Christmas. Interestingly, the leader of our prison cell got the pocketknife. Since the prison guards inspected my Backpack before they let me into the cell, they would be the ultimate owners of my "stolen" gifts.

I was given a matt and an army blanket for sleeping. However, being on the floor near the gate was drafty and too cold to sleep. I called for the guard and asked for another blanket. The guard came back about an hour later with a damp blanket that smelled like a dirty mop. I tried to sleep, but my sleep was fitful and full of bad dreams. This I recognized as a demonic attack on my person.

The next day was December 25, I was told to prepare to move to another prison early in the morning. This being the first time in prison, made it hard for me to appreciate the deplorable conditions of this particular prison.

I wondered why they would send me to a prison for just one day. One of the prisoners said it was a joke on me. The trip to the prison was a long one, and it was made longer because we stopped at a number of other jails before arriving at the Tel Aviv prison. During that long trip, I reflected as to why I was in the van with all those criminals wearing handcuffs with armed guards riding shotgun. I prayed, asking God why it was so hard to find someone to sympathize with my case.

Suddenly, I recalled how all of Jesus disciples forsook Him because they were afraid for their own welfare. I was carrying a pocket New Testament. I casually opened it, and began to read. It said, "If the world hates you, you know that it hated me before it hated you. If ye were of the world, the world would love you: but because you are not of the world, and I have chosen you out of the world, therefore the world hates you. Remember the word that I said unto you, the servant is not greater than his Lord; if they have persecuted me, they will also persecute you, if they have kept my sayings, they will keep yours also. But all these things they will do unto you for my name's sake, because they know not Him that sent me… These things I have spoken unto you, that ye should not be offended. They shall put you out of the synagogues: yea, the time cometh, that whosoever killeth you will think that he doeth God service. And these things will they do unto you because they have not known the Father, nor Me. But these things have I told you, that when the time shall come, ye may remember that I told you of them." (John 15:18 – 16:4) KJV

The Holy Spirit made this passage of Scripture very real to me, and it is now one of my most favorite passages of Scripture.

CHAPTER 10 - MIRACULOUS DREAMS AND REVEALATIONS

JUSTIFICATION

On November 9, 1997. I was studying my Bible Study Fellowship lesson nine page five where it says, "Indeed, if Peter's example was followed, the whole church of Christ would be divided and God's principles of being justified by faith alone misinterpreted."

When I read this, I immediately became suspicious for two reasons. First, I had learned many years ago that Martin Luther had added, somewhere in the Scriptures, the word "alone" after the word "faith". Second, I noticed that although the phrase "justification by faith alone" was referred to as God's principal and was in quotation marks there was no Bible reference given, and this is what made me most suspicious. I thought, if this truly is God's principal, why is there no supporting Bible reference given so that a diligent Berean Bible student would be able to search the Scriptures to confirm it?

At this juncture, I believe the Holy Spirit posed two questions. First, is there any place in the Scriptures where this principle of justification by faith alone is expressly stated? Second, is there any place in the Scriptures where the word "alone" immediately follows the word "faith"?

Using the Strong's Concordance I was led to where Paul wrote, "Therefore we conclude that a man is justified by faith without deeds of the law." Romans 3:28 KJV. I must admit that statement shocked me on first reading it because it seemed to contradict my understanding of Jesus' Sermon on the Mount where Jesus said, "Think not that I am come to destroy the law or the prophets: I am not come to destroy, but to fulfill. For verily I say unto you, till heaven and earth pass, one jot or one tittle shall in no wise pass from the law, till all be fulfilled." Matthew 5:17-21 KJV. However, when I read the context I was reassured because Paul wrote, "Do we then make void the law through faith? God forbid: yea, we establish the law." Romans 3:31 KJV.

Since I had not followed up on all the references to faith, I returned to the concordance to firmly establish whether there exist any place in the Scriptures where the word "alone" immediately follows the word "faith". Then I found in the concordance, "... man is justified, and not by faith only."

Now, since the word "only" is a synonym for the word "alone", I thought this might be the proof text for the doctrine of justification by faith alone. However, when I turn to James 2:24 and read, "Ye see then how that by works a man is justified and not by faith only." I was ecstatic! Here I was, searching the Scriptures for a proof text for the doctrine of justification by faith alone. And what do I find? The very antithesis expressly stated! How ironic! God does have a sense of humor.

The next day I was browsing in a Christian bookstore when my eye caught the name R.C. Sproul. I had heard of him recently. The title of the book was, *Grace Unknown*. When I turned to the table of contents, I found a chapter on justification. I then learned that the very same Scripture references that the Holy Spirit led me to the day before, were the very same Scripture references the Roman Catholic Church and the Reformers used as their proof texts at the Council of Trent! The Roman Catholics used James 2:24 and the Reformers used Romans 3:28. Some will say that it was a mere coincidence. But that's not all.

A short time later, when I arrived home, I came across a book that had just come in from an estate sale, the business my landlord was in. The book's title is, *True Saints*, by Charles G. Finney. I read from the dust cover, "There are two classes of self-deceivers, according to Finney, at opposite extremes of the spectrum.

There is that group which makes religion to consist altogether in outward works, and that which makes it consist altogether in faith. Both, says Finney, 'are equally false and equally fatal', those who make religion consist altogether in good works, overlook the fact that works themselves are not acceptable to God unless they proceed from faith. For, without faith it is impossible to please Him. And those who make religion consistent altogether in faith, overlook the fact that true faith always works by love, and invariably produces the works of love."

GOD MIRACULASLY SPOKE TO ME

This happened when I was in California. I was seeking God in a wilderness spot and I prayed, obeying You is so hard, why is it so hard? Then I went to sleep and had a dream. I dreamt that I was in a foot race and I was in the lead. We were running alongside the freeway, then suddenly Jesus appeared huge in white robe and His arm was pointing at us telling us to turn around and go back. So we all did an about face. Then of course I was no longer in the lead.

So I woke up and thought about the dream, but I didn't understand it. I started to hike into town. The path was narrow with a cliff on one side and a wall on the other. Suddenly, I noticed this huge Tarantula spider stopping me in my tracks. I wondered how I would get past it on the extremely narrow path. A path so narrow that if I lost my balance I could fall off the cliff to my death... I picked up some sand and threw it on the spider thinking it would run away but instead, it rose up on its legs in battle position. I had no idea how I would get past this spider when the path was so narrow and I was trapped between a wall at my right shoulder and a two hundred foot cliff to my left. I had no other choice but to get brave... so I said a prayer and jumped over the giant spider. Was this another omen?

I continued on and finally made it to the road to start hitch-hiking. The first vehicle that came along gave me a ride. Usually, I immediately ask a stranger if they are a believer in Jesus Christ but the young man giving me the ride asked me first. As we drove along, he asked me to get a book out of his

105

glove compartment so I reached in and pulled out a Bible. Right on the front of the Bible was this 3D picture of a foot race just like in my dream! Under the picture was a reference to Hebrews 12.

I was stunned. I said, "Wow! This is exactly what my dream was about last night."

The young man smiled and looked at the Bible I was holding, prodding me to read from Hebrews chapter 12. I read, "And ye have forgotten the exhortation which speaketh unto you as unto children, "My son, despise not the chastening of the Lord, nor faint when thou art rebuked of him: For whom the Lord loveth he chasteneth, and scourgeth every son whom he receiveth." Hebrews 12:5-6 KJV There was the answer to my prayer asking God why obeying Him was so hard!

The Holy Spirit reminds me that Jesus said, "Because straight is the gate and narrow is the way, which leadeth unto life, and few there be that find it." Matthew 7:14 KJV

PRAYED FOR RAIN

I was in the San Bernardino forest in my tent resting when a couple came out of nowhere shouting, "Fire! Fire!"

I asked, "Where?"

They stood by my tent with their arms full of camping gear and said, "Down at the creek a few hundred feet away. We need to get down there to put it out! Help us!"

I jumped out of the tent and looked straight up into the sky searching for some assurance that if I prayed for rain, it might rain and there was a cloud directly over-head. So I said, "While we're fighting the fire we can pray for rain." His wife joyously agreed, and we ran down to the fire.

We had nothing to fight the fire with, nor any experience in fighting fires so all we could think to do was to throw dirt on it. The fire got out of control and started burning up the side of a large Douglas Fir.

They said, "We have got to get out of here!" So we ran back to my tent. I was lacking energy and was taking my time to pack everything neatly. They, being in a panic, said no we don't have time for that. So we just threw everything on to my tent and started our hike out.

Then we began to see Helicopters landing and dropping off fire fighters. It looked just like a military operation and reminded me of my time in Vietnam. We then hit the trail to walk toward the helicopters thinking they could get us out.

When they met up with us, they asked if we knew how the fire started so we told them we saw a family down in the area not allowed for camping with an unattended campfire. So the lead fire fighter from the choppers asked us to wait there on the trail.

As we waited, we continued to pray for rain. Planes were flying over dropping water and chemicals on the fire that had grown to at least 5 acres. The man's wife suggested we sing praise songs to Jesus. As we were singing the song, "Praise You Jesus," Suddenly, we heard the fire fighters cheering, felt the air get chilly, and saw the sky get dark. The man's wife quickly pulled a tarp out of their gear and pulled it over the top of us. Rain poured down for about ten or fifteen minutes and put out the fire! We got tired of waiting for the chief fire fighter to show up so we hiked out. I set up camp again for the night and they left.

The next morning I hiked back to the site of the fire. I came upon a fire fighter called a Smokey stationed on the site. I told him that we had prayed for rain.

The Smokey said, "Had it not rained, the fire would have become a major forest fire."

I asked him, how much damage was done?

He said, "The cost was not in lost timber, but was in the cost of the airplanes to fight the fire.

UNFORGETABLE DREAM

I wanted to find a family in Christ so I went to a few American Christian ministries in hopes of finding a place of fellowship with kindred spirits. Unfortunately, I kept finding myself being rejected when I opened up to share my experiences with Jesus Christ and my desire to help widows and orphans and my desire to share the gospel of repentance and forgiveness of sins in the name of Jesus Christ.

In my dream, I was climbing a large beautiful orange tree. I searched limb after limb but I could not find a single orange. I had this dream while visiting the campus of a certain Christian ministry who's name shall remain anonymous.

When awakened I thought of how this dream reminded me of this large Christian ministry that I was visiting hoping to find guidance and fellowship. The orange tree being very large and beautiful reminded me of big beautiful Christian ministries that have lots of money but no real faith and love.

I recall that Jesus said, "Nevertheless when the Son of man cometh, shall he find faith on the earth?" Luke 18:8
I must be careful to add, lest I be misunderstood, that there are true wheat amongst the tares, but they will generally be those of low degree. I'm reminded of Isaiah 66:1-2!

STABBED IN THE BACK

I was attending a church where my Landlady was a member. She was an active member of this church, and she held a Bible study at her house that people from other affiliate churches came to.

One night, I dreamt that I went to a church and one of the members greeted me warmly and embraced me. But when he embraced me he stabbed me in the back with a sharp object which made a clear liquid flow out of me causing me to grow weak and fall down.

When I awoke, I felt like I could not trust the church or my roommate or my Landlady that hosted the home Bible study so I stopped going to both and started attending a Messianic congregation Kahela Ha Mashiah which means Congregation of the Messiah. After attending this congregation for a year, I learn that although they met on the Sabbath, the leader did not think it important to keep the Sabbath. He and I then had a falling out and I then learned that there were Messianic congregations that believed it was important to keep the Sabbath and there were those who did not think it important.

I started going to a different Messianic congregation and kept more to myself at home until I could move out two years later. I was thankful God gave me the dream to guide me in the right direction.

HATE MESSAGE ON A DOOR

I was out in the Mt. Hood wilderness praying for God to speak to me.

I woke up in the middle of the night after dreaming about a graffiti like hate message left on a poor man's door.

Then I went back to sleep and had another dream. In this dream, I was in a forested rural area and I walked out of the woods into a small village. All of the buildings were log cabins and there was one cabin in the middle of the village, it was the largest and newest. All of the other log cabins were small and run down.

I walked into the new big log cabin and there were two secretaries talking. One said, "Oh, my ink pen is not working." The other secretary said, "Oh, just throw it away, we have lots more where that came from." I had the feeling the secretaries were being wasteful.

After waking up, I didn't understand what this vivid dream meant but I knew it was not just a normal dream. God definitely had given me this dream.

A few months later, I was driving around near Klamath Falls looking for Morel mushrooms, and I accidentally locked myself out of my car. So, I took a rock and tried to break the passenger-side window but all it did was scratch the glass. I stopped to pray. And the Lord reminded me of this guy who does locks who told me that if I ever lock myself out of my car that all I would have to do is find someone driving another Japanese model car and their key would open my door but will not turn on the ignition.

So, I walked to the main highway to pretend to hitch-hike and miraculously the first car that stopped was a Japanese modeled vehicle and the person was very willing to help me. I was surprised he wasn't afraid because I took him back into the woods with the story his key could open my door. He opened my door, I was so thankful.

I traveled through many towns and county seats looking for spring mushrooms. I began to notice that every time I passed through a county seat the largest building was always the county courthouse! This reminded me of my dream where all the village log-cabins were small and run down except for one large new log cabin in the middle of the village.

Proverbs popped up in my mind. "Wealth hath many friends but the poor are hated even by their own." Pr. 19:4   Also, "How long will ye judge unjustly, and accept the persons of the wicked? Defend the poor and fatherless: do justice to the afflicted and needy. Deliver the poor and needy: rid them out of the hand of the wicked." Ps. 82:2-4 KJV

As usual, God revealed the meaning of the dream He gave me months ago. It comforted me with the reassurance that all I really need in this world is His love and He would show it in all sorts of ways like sending me the man in the Japanese made car to help me.

MY QUEST TO FIND A KINDRED SPIRIT

As the years have gone by, I have not found more than a couple of close friends who share my passion for Christ. When I pondered this, I recalled having had a severe panic attack on the side of the highway to Salinas, California almost forty years ago. I had always wondered what the scripture I randomly opened up to that day meant until now.

The scripture was Jeremiah 5:1-2 KJV which said, run ye to and fro through the streets Jerusalem, and see now, and know, and seek in the board places thereof, if ye can find a man, if there be any that execute judgement, that seek the truth: and I will pardon it. And thou they say, the Lord liveth; surely they swear falsely.

112

It means true Christians are far and few between!

So, the rejection I felt over the years was just part of being a Child of God. Ezekiel 34 KJV says, "And the Word of the Lord came unto me, saying, Son of man, prophecy against the shepherds of Israel, prophecy, and say unto them, Thus saith the Lord God unto the shepherds; Wow be to the shepherds of Israel that do feed themselves! Should not the shepherds feed the flocks? Ye eat the fat, and ye clothe you with the wool, ye kill them that are fed: but ye feed not the flock. The diseased have ye not strengthened, neither have ye healed that which was sick, neither have ye bound up that which was broken, neither have ye brought again that which was driven away, neither have ye sought that which was lost; but with force and with cruelty have ye ruled them. And they were scattered because there was no shepherd: and they became meat to all the beasts of the field, when they were scattered."

The meaning of a dream I had years ago while I was in Israel has become more clear now in my old age. I had dreamt about the time I was living in Jerusalem in a suburb called Ain Kerem and doing volunteer work at St. Vincent De Paul, a home for severely handicapped children. I dreamt that I was riding in a black coach headed to my wedding, and the handicapped children I was caring for were driving the coach. They were laughing and rejoicing while whipping the horses making the coach go very fast. I was peeking out of the couch window frightened because of pouring down rain with thunder and lightning crashing all around. The children were wearing shiny black fishermen coats. I was in the coach thinking, "I hope my bride is beautiful."

I did not understand the message in this dream then. Almost forty years later, I feel the message is that, when we help the poor and needy out of true charity, then they are driving us to The Wedding! Jesus said, "For ye have the poor always with you;" Matthew 26:11

I recall a waking vision I had a short time after my born again experience. I saw a buck deer looking down into a beautiful river valley. It reminded me of the famous story Bambi. So I went to Powell's Books down town Portland and purchased a copy. After Bambi had been shot, his father came up behind him shouting, "Run Bambi, Run!" So, Bambi ran with his father running behind encouraging him to keep on running until they could find a safe place to rest. Finally, they stopped to rest and Bambi's father left Bambi there under the log. When Bambi got out from under the log, he searched for something to eat but only found bitter herbs when suddenly his father returned. His wise father told Bambi this... "If you only learn one thing from me, learn that if you want to live long and be truly wise you must live alone."

The more time I spend with Him reading His Word and Enjoying His presence through praise and prayer, I find I am obeying the greatest commandment which is to love the Lord thy God with all your heart, mind, and soul. I find that as I obey the greatest command of Christ, I am able to obey the second command which is to love thy neighbor as thyself.

One night in the spring of 79 as I recall, I was camping out on some forest land eight miles up the south bank of the Chetco River that my parents owned. It was night and I was reading a critic by Herman Melville on Nathaniel Hawthorne by candle light. Melville was praising Hawthorne's work saying that he was America's Shakespeare. And I, being young and naïve, was eating it all up.

Suddenly I felt something on my left shoulder. At first, I thought part of my camping tarp had fallen, but when I turned my head to look, I found staring me in the face an Owl! In a fright, I turned my head forward and started shouting AHHHH! While flapping my arms as though I would fly away. Then the Owl flew silently away. I was struck by how silent the Owl's flight was. I will never forget it.

Many years later, I was led to read Tom Brown's book, *The Tracker*. I was intrigued by one chapter entitled, as I recall, *Omen*. Something he wrote, that I found especially interesting, was that if a wild animal comes near you at a normal distance then it is not an omen, but if a wild animal comes unusually close to you, then that is an omen! By this time I am feeling a leading to study this deeper. I look up the word omen and learn that it is a super natural message and at first I thought that the owl is a symbol of wisdom but then I thought wait a minute that is according to conventional wisdom. Perhaps I should search deeper. So I went on line and found that from ancient times in Egypt the owl was a symbol of DEATH! Then I recall a short time after my born again experience, I was reading, *The Minister's Black Veil*, by Nathaniel Hawthorne.

The night after reading it I had a bad dream. In the dream there was these glowing red eyes. When they came close to me I would moan with fear and pain. When I awoke I felt that the bad dream had something to do with my reading, *The Minister's Black Veil*! Now I feel the omen of the owl was a

warning that to read worldly literature is to feed upon
DEATH! But to faithfully study the Word of God is to feed
upon LIFE!

Made in the USA
Middletown, DE
16 November 2022